KENNEDY GREEN HOUSE

KENNEDY GREEN HOUSE

Designing an Eco-Healthy Home from the
Foundation to the Furniture

ROBIN WILSON

FOREWORD BY ROBERT F. KENNEDY JR.

BOOK DESIGN BY EVA GREEN & SARAH A. COHEN
PRINCIPAL PHOTOGRAPHY BY VANESSA LENZ

GREENLEAF
BOOK GROUP PRESS

Published by Greenleaf Book Group Press
Austin, Texas
www.greenleafbookgroup.com

Distributed by Greenleaf Book Group LLC

For ordering information or special discounts for bulk purchases, please contact
Greenleaf Book Group LLC at PO Box 91869, Austin, TX 78709, (512) 891-6100

Book design by Eva Green and Sarah A. Cohen
Cover design by Greenleaf Book Group LLC
Photography by Vanessa Lenz
Website: www.kennedygreenhouse.com

Publisher's Cataloging-In-Publication Data
(Prepared by The Donohue Group, Inc.)

Wilson, Robin, 1969-
   Kennedy green house : designing an eco-healthy home from the foundation to the furniture / Robin Wilson ; foreword by Robert F. Kennedy Jr. ; principal photography by Vanessa Lenz ; design by Eva Green and Sarah A. Cohen. -- 1st ed.

   p. : ill. ; cm.
   ISBN: 978-1-60832-030-1

1. Ecological houses--Design and construction. 2.Interior decoration--Environmental aspects. 3. Ecological houses--Health aspects. 4. Sustainable design. 5. Dwellings--Environmental engineering. 5. Kennedy, Robert Francis, 1954---Homes and haunts--New York (State)--Westchester County. I. Kennedy, Robert Francis, 1954- II. Lenz, Vanessa. III. Green, Eva and Cohen, Sarah A. IV. Title.

TH4860 .W55 2010
690/.047   2010920228

Part of the Tree Neutral™ program, which offsets the number of trees consumed in the production and printing of this book by taking proactive steps, such as planting trees in direct proportion to the number of trees used:
www.treeneutral.com

Printed in Canada on acid-free paper

10 11 12 13 14 10 9 8 7 6 5 4 3 2 1

First Edition

Dedicated to the memory of
my brother Russel (1971 - 1993)
and to my parents.

ACKNOWLEDGMENTS

The completion of the Kennedy Green House project was possible due to the singular focus of a team of professionals who, in the face of many challenges, never faltered. The chapters in the book will tell you more about the leadership from the architects, the builder, the project manager, and others. The project was also possible due to the energetic and focused team members at Robin Wilson Home (Kelli Thornwell, Caitlyn Fitzgerald, Lisa Marie Scotti and Theresa Puchkoff) who worked with the client to complete CAD drawings, to create material schedules and to find sponsors who were willing to donate during a year of economic adversity. Finally, our team worked diligently to ensure that the sponsors were pleased with media and product placement upon completion. All the sponsors who participated are to be thanked profusely—as the home would not have been completed without their involvement—and we appreciate the message they are conveying to global consumers that "eco-friendly can be beautiful."

Thank you to those friends who tried to get me out of the office before midnight during the past year. Your words and encouragement were touchstones throughout the project in the face of some adversity. Thank you to the Board, Investors and Advisors whose support, emails, and phone calls were and will remain priceless.

And a heartfelt thank-you to those who helped me build my foundation long
before we began this project. Those who believed in me, and my dream
(and I apologize in advance if I miss a name, but you know who you are!):
Johnny & Diane Scott, Jerry Lawson, Connie Lucas, John Hall,
Cheryl Dorsey, Joy Touchstone, Pam Everhart, Sandra Sims-Williams,
Irma Tyler-Wood, Bennie & Flash Wiley, Ray Shepard, Ilene Lush,
Imal Wagner, Jeanne Noonan Eckholdt, Michael Clinton, Alana Frumkes,
Jim Offutt, Monique Ruff-Bell, Renee Warren, Christy & John Mack,
Zaid Abdul Aleem, Peg Treadwell, Kiki & Emanuel Monogenis, Vince Hodshire,
Vinny Castiello, Helen Robinson, Jesse Cameron Glickenhaus, Majora Carter,
Darryl Wash, Patrick Croke, Dave Dooley, Byron Harmon, Stephanie Cassell,
Charlie Rose, Janice Goldfinger, Cari Modine, Trish Jones, Todd Weber,
Jamie Kwiat, Jenny Cross, Esther Perman, Lisa Jasper, Jehudith Cohen,
Ginny Bachman, Kim Bourus, Gloria Reuben, Nina & Kevin King, Julie Gaines,
Mary Galvin, Paul Zemitzsch, Alan Laytner, Scott Shafranek, Matthew Sheehy,
Mike Kenny, Dennis Jeter and so many others . . .

And thank you to Laura Turner Seydel and Amanda Leesburg, who introduced me
to this client and project. Thank you for your invaluable advice and for showing
me EcoManor!

And a priceless thank-you to Patterson Belknap Webb Tyler, and our lawyers—
Peter Harvey and Andy Beame—whose support of our firm has been amazing.
I look forward to many more years of working with your stellar team and firm . . .

CONTENTS

FOREWORD

ROBERT F. KENNEDY JR.

In 2003, my family was enjoying a Cape Cod vacation when a deluge inundated our Mt. Kisco, New York, home, a sprawling clapboard 1920 structure astride an 1870 stone foundation—all treacherously encased in 1950s era aluminum siding. Standing water from the flood caused a black mold bloom that, thriving in the moisture trapped inside by the building's metallic skin, colonized in the upper stories as though in a petri dish. The children fell sick, and our every effort to remove the mold failed. Nevertheless, when visitors with hacking coughs fled our home for fresh air, I taunted them from the front steps to come back and "man up." We fought a two-year losing battle against the creeping fungus. Finally, in 2005, after unsuccessfully attempting a gut renovation, we realized the only solution was to raze and rebuild.

Although sad about losing our century-old family home, I was excited by the prospect of building a green house. For twenty-five years I've been a professional environmental advocate, working as an attorney for Riverkeeper and the Natural Resources Defense Council, as the founder and president of the Waterkeeper Alliance, and as a professor of environmental litigation at Pace Law School. In these endeavors I have filed and fought more than four hundred lawsuits against polluters while simultaneously lobbying for, speaking around the world on, and writing about environmental topics. I figured it was about time I started walking the walk in my own home.

I felt well equipped to handle the task and worked with my wife, Mary Richardson—who had been an architect for over two decades and worked at the design firm Parish-Hadley. Mary worked on the renovation of the Naval Observatory in Washington, D.C., the official residence of then Vice President of the United States Al Gore. She was therefore eager to turn her talents to greening her own crib.

Since 2005, I've served on the board of VantagePoint Venture Partners, the nation's largest green tech venture capital firm with a mission to develop green tech businesses in the renewable energy sources and energy efficiency spheres. I've come to believe that innovative green technologies offer the best hope for saving the planet, and for building prosperous, dignified, enriching, healthy, and sustainable communities for our children.

Harnessing efficiency and America's abundant stable of such renewable sources as wind, solar, geothermal, tidal, and biomass energy could quickly free our country from its deadly addictions to oil and coal. I was stoked to use my home as a showcase for cutting-edge technologies and as a proving ground for the "new energy" economy.

Our objectives were sixfold: to bolster energy efficiency and rely on power generated on-site; to reduce solid waste; to improve air and water quality; to protect and enhance our local environment; to conserve natural resources; and, of course, to build a healthier home for our children.

COST

Homeowners frequently fail to take advantage of the many tax breaks and incentives offered by state and federal governments for building LEED-certified homes or adding green features. People who live in green houses save money by consuming less energy and less water than standard homes and suffering fewer days of missed work from illnesses. Green homes are more durable than conventional structures and require fewer repairs. Soon, it will cost less to insure a green home than a standard home. An increasing number of insurance and mortgage companies already offer discounted coverage and loan rates for home buyers purchasing green. Finally, green home resale values are far higher than those of comparable standard homes.

But we expect our most dramatic cost savings to come from reducing the enormous operating costs of our former home with its inefficient oil heat compounded by poor insulation, leaking windows, a sieve-like ventilation system, and endless repairs. When we began construction, we acted on the principle that any innovative technologies would have to have a quick payback—under five years.

DEMOLITION

Consistent with her antipathy toward disposables, Mary made sure that after its demolition, the old house was recycled 100 percent. Demolition of a standard 2,500-square-foot home creates approximately two tons of construction waste that ends up in landfills. Mary found an extraordinary company called Green Demolitions that dismantled, recycled, or sold the entire house to scrap dealers, manufacturers, and developers. Not a single nail, mantle, stud, or tile fragment went to a landfill. In a patented process, the firm pulverized our old mold-infested sheetrock and sold the purified material to gypsum manufacturers to create new sheetrock. We actually received a substantial tax break for donating the proceeds of recovered materials to a Catskill-based nonprofit drug rehab facility supported by Green Demolitions.

RECYCLED MATERIALS

We reused the studs and girders from our old home. We collected stone debris from blasting out the basement and used it to construct our porch. With the help of world-famous green architect Allan Shope, we harvested roof tiles from a demolished mental institution in Wassaic. My children, accustomed to the bedlam of our home, often remind me how appropriate it is that we will literally live beneath the reclaimed roof of a former insane asylum.

WATER

Innovative water control devices allow us to limit water use—important since we live in the New York City reservoir watershed. The built environment accounts for about 14 percent of potable water consumption in our country. We remind our children that everything that goes down our toilet or bathtub drain ends up pouring through someone else's faucet in Manhattan. We like to think that our waste water goes to the midtown office of greedy corporate lawyers.

DESIGN

Mary was inspired by the designs of Mott B. Schmidt and worked with two architects, Brooks Washburn and Patrick Croke (plus consulting regularly with Allan Shope), initially on a weekly basis, and later a monthly basis. The team collaborated to design a classically elegant structure that blends perfectly with the landscape and character of our community.

And Mary hired Robin Wilson, an eco-friendly design pioneer, who was a key part of securing sponsors to become a part of this project. Without her team, our home would not have secured over $1 million in donations from the sponsors. We are also thrilled that the Robin Wilson Home custom eco-cabinetry is installed in our home in three locations!

LIGHTING

My home is one example of the newest trend— eco-friendly buildings that are tightly insulated, have super-efficient lighting and appliances, and are powered by geothermal and solar panels. By switching to LED lights we will save on electricity. By replacing a standard 60-watt bulb with an LED that gives the same light (800 lumeres) and typically burns for 1,100 hours each year, my family will save about 66 kilowatt hours each year on each lightbulb. In New York, where we pay about 13 cents per kilowatt hour, that's $8.58 a year in savings for each of the fifty-five light bulbs in our home, or a total of $472. The annual cost savings for some homeowners could reach into the thousands.

It has occurred to me that ours is not just a home— *we have constructed a power plant* that will allow us to participate, as a family, in the new energy economy while minting enormous cost savings. We've indicated to our children that within a few years, new laws will allow us to actually sell all of our surplus back to the grid at market rates and thus make enough money to pay for their college funds. In the meantime, we're urging them to apply to state schools.

OUR COUNTRY

Green is the new red, white, and blue. We are proud to be participating in an economy that will soon free our country from a deadly addiction to foreign oil and toxic coal. Self-sufficiency in the energy sector is a patriotic duty of every American. It will improve our national security and preserve our country from periodic oil wars and the dependence that has our country funding both sides of the war on terror.

Moreover, a distributed power system owned by tens of millions of American homeowners is not only more democratic than a power system controlled by a few wealthy plutocrats; it is more reliable, more resilient, and far less vulnerable to attack by our enemies. It's a simple thing for a terrorist to blow up a power plant, but far trickier to blow up a million homes operating as power plants.

Coal is just as bad for America as oil is, and it remains the most prolific source of this nation's greenhouse gases. The slick ad campaign financed by powerful coal firms might claim that coal is cheap and clean, but the reality is this: Ozone and particulates from coal plants kill tens of thousands of Americans each year and cause widespread illnesses and disease.

- Acid rain from coal stacks has destroyed millions of acres of valuable forests and sterilized one in five Adirondack lakes.

- Neurotoxic mercury raining from these plants has contaminated every freshwater fish in the USA and poisons 1 million-plus American women and children annually.

- Coal industry strip mines have already destroyed 500 mountains in Appalachia, buried 2,000 miles of rivers and streams, and will soon have flattened an area the size of Delaware.

We should be using our natural renewable resources. Our biggest potential for low-cost megawatts will come from the energy savings—or "negawatts"— we get from exploiting all the hidden opportunities for efficiency in our built environment.

I hope that you learn from our family's experience and find a way to incorporate some of these techniques into your own home. Everyone can profit from the green gold rush. And by greening your own crib, you can help our country solve our most urgent national problems—global warming, security, a staggering debt, and a stagnant economy.

Robert F. Kennedy, Jr.
FALL 2009

Bust of Robert F. Kennedy on living room mantle.

PREFACE

ROBIN WILSON

Since my firm began, our mantra has been "eco-friendly can be beautiful" from the foundation to the furniture. It is the belief of Robin Wilson Home that to have an eco-friendly space, you must start with an understanding of the products that are inserted into the walls, materials used for the flooring, and finishes/adhesives used in cabinetry and furniture. Without this knowledge, you can inadvertently create a beautiful home that has toxins built in . . . and given that your home is your ecosystem, a little bit of knowledge is priceless.

As a leading pioneer in eco-friendly design, Robin Wilson Home is on a mission to provide eco-healthy educational information and material specification options for both residential and commercial spaces. A key element of my motivation for accepting this project was the fact that the client was committed to environmentally-friendly design. After learning about their children's health issues due to the mold contamination, my empathy was quite strong, as I grew up with and continue to be affected by both allergies and asthma. Early memories as a child include watching my parents remove the plush shag carpeting in our home and returning to exposed hardwood floors, tile, and area rugs. These simple solutions will also be part of the Kennedy home design.

In my first job as a college intern at the Lower Colorado River Authority, we explored technologies such as demand side management (DSM), where nonessential appliances could be cycled off during peak demand in multifamily buildings. Interestingly, this technology is just starting to be used now in residential construction, almost twenty years later!

My firm has a philosophy of "eco-friendliness from the foundation to the furniture" and we worked to make sure that sustainable practices and materials were installed in the house. These sustainable platforms are showcased throughout the Kennedy home, from the recycled resources used for building (slate, timber, flooring) to the salvaged and refurbished (furniture).

An amazing team of professionals believed in and shared our mission, and that sustained us as we faced many challenges throughout this project. We suggested many innovations to the Kennedy family such as Solatubes, Somnium mattresses and our eco-friendly cabinetry line. The Kennedys were always willing to consider technology innovation and options. Working with the building-architecture-design team, there were many amazing suggestions—and together we have created a "living laboratory" in a home that will be the cutting edge

in the eco-movement. After our team meetings—with everyone from the builder to the architects to the project manager—to learn more about the family's individual and collective needs, we were prepared to build and design a home for both informal and formal entertaining.

It should be emphasized that most families will not have the luxury of assembling a team like this for their project, but this book will provide a template to educate on best-practice options available for your project.

> It is our belief that everyone deserves an eco-healthy space, no matter their level of income.

Our goal was to take a toxic home covered with black mold and turn it into an eco-healthy space. Designing a home with reclaimed materials, sustainable options and beautiful products required focus on the basic goals—limit wheezing and sneezing—while still focusing on cost-effective and high-efficiency options available on the market.

Our hope is that with more awareness, consumers will push supply and demand to the point where eco-friendly building practices become standard so that at some point, these eco-healthy options will be affordable for all families, no matter their level of income. It is important to know that the Kennedy family—just like you—had to follow a budget. Throughout the project, choices had to be made accordingly. In fact, one of the client's most exciting moments was watching the meter *run backward* when the photovoltaic solar panel system was turned on.

The four principles of eco-friendly design that our firm follows are: sustainable, reusable, recyclable and non-toxic. Lately, we have seen trends toward a return to traditional building methods, with a twist: the insulation may be recycled blue jeans or newspapers; the flooring may be reclaimed from old barns; and the lighting may be high-efficiency LED or fiber optic. From the aesthetic beauty of organic and sustainable textiles; to cork or bamboo flooring; to no-to-low VOC paints; it is our belief that consumers are more excited than ever about the array of building materials.

The Kennedy home is powered by alternative energy sources including geothermal, solar panels, hybrid hot water heaters and radiant floors, and is heated and cooled by one of the most efficient systems. The Kennedys continually reminded us to remember Bobby's work as an environmentalist and to use the house as a showcase for some of these cutting-edge technologies—but they also wanted the home to be "beautiful, practical, comfortable,

all on a disciplined budget." The family told us that they were once the largest customers of the propane company, and they wanted to see dramatic cost savings come from lower energy usage. Their original 1920 home had inefficient oil heat, compounded with poor insulation, ill-fitting windows and breezy clapboard construction. This newly constructed, masonry home will open your eyes to classic architectural design using the multiple eco-options available today. And who can imagine what the future will bring in the field of eco-friendly space?

Thanks to the multiple sponsors who took my calls and contributed to the Kennedy Green House. This home is a "living laboratory" that showcases today's cutting-edge technology and eco-friendly options at varied price points. Our ultimate goal is to allow designers, architects, builders, and consumers to be exposed to eco-friendly possibilities. Consumers will hopefully begin to embrace this mindset for their homes and offices, so supply and demand will create cost efficiencies.

We hope that by viewing this book, reviewing the resource guide and utilizing the green pages, you will enable the suppliers and sponsors who participated in this project to continue to showcase their leadership in the eco-friendly space.

Your secret peek into the Kennedy home begins now. Please enjoy the experience.

Robin Wilson
FALL 2009

SITE & BACKSTORY

CHAPTER 1

The Kennedys' home sits on a twelve-acre plot of land with the rear façade facing a thirty-acre private lake. The first thing we noticed is that this property is home to wetlands, forest, waterfront and rocky terrain. This homesite is a perfect place to live when you are environmentally aware—there is everything from turtles to fishing to bird and bat nesting habitats—and want to see your impact on the ecosystem.

When the family purchased the house, they became the third owners of a site that was originally used and built by the Scribner publishing family as their summer cottage. The home was commissioned in 1908 and built by 1920 by Arthur H. Scribner and designed by the Carrère & Hastings architecture firm, the same firm that designed the New York Public Library and the Frick Museum. With great foresight, Hastings preached that "architects ought to make use of modern engineering achievements . . . and use local materials."

OPPOSITE (clockwise from top left): Garage, birdcage, 30-acre lake, Sears & Roebuck modular home after storm.

ABOVE: Original cottage from rear and side.

In addition to the main house structure, called the cottage, there were three outbuildings: a six-car garage, an abandoned greenhouse, a modular home, plus a 9-foot birdcage. The main structure was primarily used in the summer. Unlike modern practices with central air-conditioning, the practice at the time was to build summer homes with wide wall cavities and very little insulation, to ensure that rooms stayed as cool as possible in the summer months.

In the 1950s, the second owner installed one of the first Sears & Roebuck modular homes in Westchester County. This modular home was used by the servants and later for storage. Sadly, this structure was crushed by a fallen tree during a windstorm in early 2009, during the rebuilding of the home. The family plans to rebuild a new modular home on the property at a later date, which will link the "past to the present," showcasing new and efficient technologies within the modular homebuilding sector.

We were told that the second homeowner was a famous gardener who designed manicured gardens. This landscaping, however, has slowly yielded to the Kennedys' rough-and-tumble weekend games of capture-the-flag when family, friends and neighbors join in a boisterous game throughout the grounds.

In 2003, the property was home to six children, two parents, various pets, and a live-in housekeeper, plus additional non-live-in staff. Each summer, the family travels to Hyannis Port, Massachusetts, to spend time with extended family and friends. Typically, someone would remain behind to care

Appearance of black mold in home.

for their home. However, the summer of 2003 was the exception. Upon returning home in August, the Kennedys found the remnants of a flood, with six inches of water still standing in the basement crawl space. The summer heat combined with the moisture created the perfect environment for mold infestation.

By Labor Day, toxic black mold had begun infesting every surface of the home. Unbeknownst to our client, the interior walls (because of their lack of insulation) had been overtaken by black mold. Most people don't realize that mold feeds on the paper backing of drywall (today, there are new drywall innovations that are paperless) Although measures were taken to arrest the spread of the mold, such as scrubbing down the walls with a solution of bleach and water, the experts knew that even if visible mold was cleared away and the house was completely aired out, there was a

need for continued dehumidification. So, they purchased industrial-strength dehumidifiers. Everything that could not be washed or detoxified had to be thrown away, including clothing, carpets and upholstered furniture. And mold continued its silent climb inside the walls, to the second-level sleeping quarters.

That winter, the family hoped the winter cold would kill the mold, but the problem simply intensified. After the heat was turned on, the family realized something was terribly wrong. The mold spores had entered the heating units, and began to invisibly blow back into the home, causing wheezing and sneezing among the children and to any visitors with a mold sensitivity. The severity of the situation was not fully understood until the children began to have repeated hospitalizations for pneumonia, asthma attacks, and allergen symptoms. The Kennedy parents also noticed that when they traveled, the health of the children improved. But when the family returned home, the symptoms affecting the children worsened.

The insurance company warned the Kennedys that the mold might return when the weather warmed up again. By the spring of 2005, with the warm weather returning, the mold came back with a vengeance. According to the U.S. Environmental Protection Agency (EPA), "Some people are sensitive to molds. For these people, exposure to molds can cause symptoms such as nasal stuffiness, eye irritation, wheezing, or skin irritation. Some people, such as those with serious allergies to molds, may have more severe reactions, which may include fever and shortness of breath. Some people with chronic lung illnesses, such as obstructive lung disease, may develop mold infections in their lungs."

By the summer of 2005, it was obvious that a decision had to be made on how to attempt removal of the black mold.

One option was to kill the mold using herbicides (a highly toxic substance used to kill unwanted plants). Yet, the Kennedys opted against this strategy due to the carcinogenic effects, which were too risky for the children—especially the youngest ones—in the home. Soon thereafter, the experts gave the family multiple opinions, and they decided that decision-making could occur when the children were in a safe environment. Says Bobby, "We fought a two year losing battle against the creeping fungus . . . after unsuccessfully attempting a gut renovation, we realized the only solution was to raze and rebuild."

Molds reproduce by producing tiny spores that waft through indoor and outdoor air continually. When mold spores land on a damp spot indoors, they may begin to grow by digesting whatever they are growing on in order to survive. Mold growth will often occur indoors in areas where excessive moisture or water accumulates, particularly if the moisture problem remains undiscovered or unaddressed. The key to mold control is moisture control.

Ten Things
You Should Know About Mold and
How to Control It

Excerpted list from U.S. EPA website regarding mold control.

1. Potential health effects and symptoms associated with mold exposures include allergic reactions, asthma, and other respiratory complaints.
2. There is no practical way to eliminate all mold and mold spores in the indoor environment; the way to control indoor mold growth is to control moisture.
3. If mold is a problem in your home or school, you must clean up the mold and eliminate sources of moisture.
4. Fix the source of the water problem or leak to prevent mold growth.
5. Reduce indoor humidity (to 30-60 percent) to decrease mold growth by: venting bathrooms, dryers, and other moisture-generating sources to the outside; using air conditioners and dehumidifiers; increasing ventilation; and using exhaust fans whenever cooking, dishwashing, and cleaning.
6. Clean and dry any damp or wet building materials and furnishings within 24-48 hours to prevent mold growth.
7. Clean mold off hard surfaces with water and detergent, and dry completely. Absorbent materials such as ceiling tiles, that are moldy, may need to be replaced.
8. Prevent condensation: reduce the potential for condensation on such cold surfaces as windows, piping, exterior walls, roof, or floors by adding insulation.
9. In areas where there is a perpetual moisture problem (e.g., by drinking fountains, by classroom sinks, or on concrete floors with leaks or frequent condensation), do not install carpeting.
10. Molds can be found almost anywhere; they can grow on virtually any substance, providing that moisture is present. Certain molds can grow on wood, paper, carpet, and foods.

For more information, visit: http://www.epa.gov/mold/

PLANNING TO REBUILD

CHAPTER 2

As aforementioned, getting this project off the ground involved assembling a "Green Dream Team" of highly qualified professionals. Each person was hand-selected by the client for his or her unique set of skills or relationships. We all reduced our fees for this project because we believed in the premise of creating a LEED-certified home for the Kennedys. The next step prior to building the home was the local Building Department sign-off on the team of architects' final plans. Once an approved architectural plan permit was in hand, the Blansfield Builders team went to work, bringing in a strong team of tradesmen to build the home, with a goal of one year from the ground up.

The client wanted a collaborative process, with all trade disciplines involved, throughout the entire architectural and design phase of the project. The team met for many months in a committee setting to finalize the Kennedy Green House. At the weekly and monthly meetings, discussions centered on such topics as design of the exterior brick pattern, stair rail, interior elevations, crown molding profile, building codes, bath tile layouts, and kitchen design. In many standard projects, the exterior and interior architectural plans are completed with separate involvement from the design, lighting, and plumbing teams.

FIRST STEPS

The family committed at the outset to build a green home and recognized that upfront costs are sometimes higher for green construction. Reasons for increased costs include the reality that some homebuilders and trade professionals fail to effectively plan and design a project.

In the meantime, the family transferred to a friend's vacant home that was less than a mile away from the job site. This friend was also kind enough to recommend an architect she had worked with on a previous project. And over several weeks, they packed a lifetime's worth of papers and family heirlooms into every crevice of the rental home— from the basement to the attic.

The first step was to approach an architect and hire a project manager to represent the family. Then began research into local builders who understood the green building process and interior designers who understood eco-friendly and LEED protocols. With the expertise of the client, and consultations with architects and colleagues, the builder came up with a construction figure.

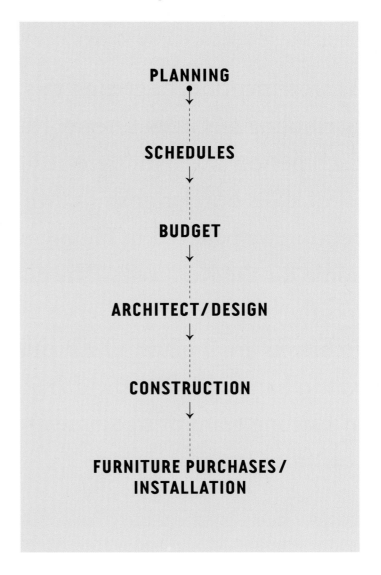

PLANNING

SCHEDULES

BUDGET

ARCHITECT/DESIGN

CONSTRUCTION

FURNITURE PURCHASES/
INSTALLATION

BILL MAYO, *Project Manager*

PROJECT MANAGER

The Kennedys hired Bill Mayo as their project manager, and he served as the liaison between the client, builder, architect and designer, and also managed logistics and conducted research. When he was hired, he ensured that no demolition was done prior to rebuilding approval from the Building Department. The complex building codes and rules were clear about the hard facts: the septic system could not be relocated because of the wetlands on the property. And if they replaced the septic system, it would mean that the structure could not be grandfathered in under new building codes. The bottom line is: had the demolition occurred prior to receiving a permit, the Kennedys would have been allowed to rebuild only a two-bedroom cottage, which would have been wholly inadequate for their family.

Says Bill, "As project manager, I worked with the client, designer, architect, builder, LEED consultants and other professionals to ensure that all the moving parts of this project were properly coordinated. My role was to oversee the project as a whole and anticipate how design changes, budget considerations or challenging field conditions would affect the whole project—and then provide insight into solutions to complement the design and satisfy the needs of the client. In addition, throughout the project, I was instructed to keep an eye out for ways to keep our building practices as sustainable as possible—using recycled and non-toxic materials and reducing waste."

ARCHITECTS

Patrick Croke, one of the architects, says, "My role on this project was to work with an incredible group of consultants to refine, adjust and create design details to make a very technology driven project more consistent with and appropriate for the historic architectural landscape of the town. While the initial goal was to construct in an environmentally friendly manner and to conserve our resources, the ultimate result is the creation of a habitat that is better for the family—for their bodies and minds—and architecture that can exist more naturally within our environment. We worked within the limitations and came up with great solutions."

And lead architect Brooks Washburn says, "Our firm is the architect of record for the project, and we were involved from the early stages of planning and design, plus construction documents and throughout the construction. We have all been helping to translate the clients' ideas and goals into a final building solution. In a general sense, the key contribution has been to house a potentially high-tech, energy-efficient structure into a home with a traditional appearance. Our main interest was the building performance—as it operates and as it is lived in. Our team designed the home to have the potential to approach zero-net-energy state with its own solar electricity and domestic hot water and ground-source heating/cooling system."

PATRICK CROKE, *Architect*

BROOKS WASHBURN, *Architect*

The client, a trained architect having worked on previous projects, was the thought leader. In weekly meetings from October 2008 to May 2009 in the dining room of the rental home or at the job site, we discussed points with openness, and collaborative input, questions, requests and suggestions. After a certain point, the project team became smaller—with architects, project manager, builder and designer—becoming the core group reporting to the client. By the end of the project, the client had transitioned to an even smaller core team of the builder and designer who continued to work on implementation of decisions.

Throughout the project, the collaboration of many parties remained integral to the project's direction and final decisions.

Throughout the project, the collaboration of many parties—who offered expert analysis, opinions, and advice—remained integral to the project's direction and final decisions. The client requested weekly meetings and progress reports. Every week for more than six months, the entire team met with the client.

At one point, the client borrowed a book from the public library which showed the work of the late society architect, Mott B. Schmidt (1889-1977), who coincidentally happens to be the grandfather of one of the Kennedy family relatives! The client was inspired by his Neo-Georgian style, which focused on elegant and sophisticated spaces. He was best known for the Gracie Mansion ballroom, along with the private homes of many aristocratic families.

When the architects began to collaborate, they drew the Kennedy home as a center-hall colonial with masonry construction and simple design detail specifications, such as a coin detail on the façade and large fireplaces in the gathering rooms. Two architectural firms—Brooks Washburn (exterior and mechanicals) and Patrick Croke (exterior and interior details)—were hired to be part of the team, with gratis consultation from a neighbor: architect Allan Shope, who is world-renowned for his green building innovations. And precisely because of their interaction and collaboration, the home has turned out with a multitude of great features.

JIM BLANSFIELD, *Builder*

BUILDER

Jim Blansfield was selected to be the builder of the home, and he is certified by the U.S. Green Building Council as a LEED-accredited professional with green building credentials. When his team was hired and learned the permit limitations would have allowed a smaller structure, he recognized that the only alternative to rebuild the home was one of the most expensive options—namely, tearing down 45 percent of the old house and then perching the remaining second story on hydraulic stilts (reaching almost as high as the children's treehouse). Then, construction began on the new house underneath the existing second-level home, while the hydraulic stilts kept the workers from danger.

Jim Blansfield says, "This project demanded the utmost of skills by all members of the team, from careful reconstruction and salvage of materials used from other sites as well as our own, to integration with the latest technology to ensure low cost energy usage and minimal maintenance over time. The end product is a proud model of what our homes should strive to be." Jim attended almost every meeting and brought along specific suppliers—from stonemasons to window and hardware experts—who could push the process forward and answer client questions.

LEED CONSULTANT

To meet the LEED protocol requirements, a third-party verification firm, Steven Winter Associates, was hired to become a key observer of the project. Providing checklists for compliance, conducting regular site reviews, and consulting frequently with the client meant that the LEED points were accumulated and tallied properly. Says Steven Winter, "Energy-efficient construction practices are an obvious and easy approach to building. High-end expensive materials are not necessary, but a focus on a tight building shell and low-VOC materials make for low-cost heating and cooling in a comfortable, healthy home."

STEVEN WINTER, *LEED Consultant*

DEMOLITION

In order to facilitate less demolition waste going to the landfills, the family worked with Green Demolitions. Says Bobby, "Demolition of a standard 2,500 sf home creates approximately two tons of construction waste that ends up in landfills." According to the statistics, over 30% of waste going to U.S. landfills is from demolished buildings. One of the unique patented processes of the Green Demolitions firm is the pulverization of the mold infested sheetrock into purified gypsum which is then resold to manufacturers to create new sheetrock. This sustainability model allows homeowners to receive a tax benefit for donating the proceeds of the recovered material to a non-profit drug rehabilitation facility.

Green Demolitions founder and president, Steve Feldman, explains his environmentally friendly philosophy this way: "Reducing project costs makes eco-sense: if you throw it out before its time, you are unnecessarily harming the environment. It also makes good sense: it's a better deal for all to reuse than to destroy. And we had two roles in this project—recycling and reuse." According to Steve, the project has been completed due to our "against all odds" attitude. "We started the project the morning of an ice storm with ten members of the team—removal crews, truckers, packers and labelers. We worked into the night and returned for several more days of recycling—and in the end over 700 items were recycled."

ROBIN WILSON, *Interior Designer*

INTERIOR DESIGNER

The Robin Wilson Home team was hired for our expertise in eco-friendly interior design. Our team goal throughout this project was to ensure that those who visit the home will begin to be exposed to eco-friendly design options, to learn about LEED principles and to showcase best practices for renovation projects. Given my personal medical history of asthma and allergies, we understood exactly what the Kennedy children were going through. As a result, we worked "from the foundation to the furniture" to design this eco-healthy home.

Plus, the client asked my design team to start asking major companies to become sponsors for durable goods, such as paint, windows, flooring and lights, among other products. The client wanted to ensure that costs could be lowered for their budget and that the companies could be featured in this living laboratory.

When we had conversations with sponsors, we helped them understand that their contribution to the project would showcase the accessibility and beauty of the eco-innovations in the marketplace.

BREAKING GROUND

After the demolition, the Blansfield Builders team broke ground in fall of 2008 with a goal of laying the foundation before it became too cold. Again, the family made sure to minimize use of virgin materials in construction. With the strong commitment of the family to sustainable practices, we had a mandate and tried to follow it through-out the project.

Says the family, "We tried to principally use salvaged materials recovered from demolished buildings. We reused the studs and girders from our old home. We collected stone debris from blasting out the basement and used it to construct our porch."

CLIENT MEETINGS

By October 2008, the team consisted of architect, builder, project manager, designer and other trades as needed. We began holding weekly design meetings with the client at the rental home. These meetings were typically held on Fridays and lasted six to eight hours. Topics included detailed plan review, building department discussions, progress reports, design layout, concept assessment and Q&A to understand the client's wishes. These collaborative meetings included free-flowing discussions—between client, architects, builder and design team. Often, these team members worked many hours after the meeting to interpret the decisions and direction from the meetings.

ECONOMIC COLLAPSE

Due to the reality of building a new foundation underneath the old home, there was a substantial increase in the budget. Later these extra costs for engineering would become more of an issue with regard to the construction and design budget as the global economy declined.

Our client was faced with building a new house, maintaining carrying costs for the original property and living in a rental home. Yet building had to go on . . . even as the global financial services market was imploding.

To assist our client with the economic situation, our team made calls to potential sponsors over many months. The Robin Wilson Home team added value both as an eco-designer and by creating sponsored product donation relationships, ultimately securing over $1.3 million in durable goods for the client— items such as Solatubes, fireplaces, toilets, tubs, sinks, faucets, paint, flooring, kitchen cabinetry, hybrid hot water heater, appliances, countertops and tile, among other things.

THE PLAN

The design team began the process by asking the client to create a wish list (within a budget) specifically outlining the features they wanted their home to possess. In addition to the list, the client outlined favorite brands and preferences for certain elements, such as ensuring that the new home should feel warm and welcoming, not formal or antiseptic.

The Kennedys remain staunch environmentalists and advocates of the Americans with Disabilities Act, and insisted that the home include ADA-compliant features and energy-efficient measures such as an access ramp, curbless shower and elevator.

Our design team typed meticulous schedules for the client for each decision area of the home. These design schedules included room finishes, paint selections, millwork, lighting, countertops, tile, flooring and fixtures. These detailed schedules assisted the team in organizing design elements on a room-by-room basis. At a certain point, due to budget, some of these specifications changed.

By using three-dimensional computer-aided design (CAD), the architect and design team was able to create floor plans, layouts, and renderings online, with revisions also sent via e-mail. This ensured that the client could review something online, but pages did not have to be printed unless needed. And at the end of the project, a final printout could be made with materials and schedules.

Our clients maintain busy schedules that require them to travel and make public appearances. The result was that on occasion, they were unavailable for on-site meetings for several weeks. Yet with

constant communication (multiple times a day!) the Green Dream Team kept the project moving forward by continuing our collaboration, speaking to vendors, and getting samples to the project manager for client review.

By the middle of the rebuilding process, we watched the global economy crumble and the client began reassessing the budget. Within a short time, our design mandate was revised and clarified. With no design budget, we worked to stage the home as a showhouse for the book and to maintain marketing commitments. We needed to please product sponsors—to ensure that they could get photography in furnished rooms—for their marketing campaigns. The Kennedy home was the perfect stage. This book will serve as the client "look book." Over time, the client will be able to acquire pieces for their home that are appropriate for their needs and budget.

Designing a home like this involves utilizing historical and vintage furniture, family artwork and unique taxidermy. As well, we wanted to find reclaimed items and sustainable new pieces, plus great accessories. The perfect balance of "modern with a classic touch," is how we define our design style. In fact, all of the items in their home had been previously photographed by the insurance team, including artwork and heirlooms. This detailed insurance document became our catalog when we were reviewing items to determine their inclusion into the home for the staged photography. It made it much easier to determine what should fit where, and it was also an opportunity to review multiple items at one time, without having to go into a storage area.

Throughout this project, we were able to assist the client by obtaining project donations from companies who believe this "living laboratory" is a necessity so that people can have a tactile experience and see, touch and feel the unique elements of this home. The open house tours of the home after the completion of construction will allow interior designers, architects, builders and product sponsors into the home to experience a perfect amalgam of eco-friendly technologies.

ABOVE: Examples of family taxidermy, including a komodo dragon and "Mr. Carruthers," RFK Jr.'s childhood pet turtle.

LIVING ROOM

CONCEPT

Use existing upholstered sofas, chairs, side tables and piano.
Gas fireplace by Majestic; flooring by John Yarema; hearth by Amendola. Install custom mantle and bookcases. Sophisticated and understated elegance.

FAMILY ROOM

CONCEPT

Sofa and upholstered chairs from Mitchell Gold + Bob Williams; factory table from ABC Home;
vintage side tables and lamps by Housing Works; nesting tables from VivaTerra; vintage flag from client
and wool sisal carpet by Karastan. Bamboo flooring by Dragonfly. Durable and functional for heavy use.

MASTER BEDROOM

CONCEPT

Upholstered headboard and railing by Mitchell Gold + Bob Williams;
organic cotton linens, blanket chest from client; accessories from client and Housing Works; artwork from
client; custom mantle; gas fireplace by Majestic; flooring by Mohawk; hearth by Amendola.
Relaxing and simple master bedroom space.

GUEST BEDROOM

CONCEPT

FSC wood headboard; organic cotton linens; vintage side tables from client; lamps from The Nest Store; artwork from client. Retreat for guests.

BOY'S BEDROOM

CONCEPT

Reclaimed barnwood bed and headboard by VivaTerra; organic cotton linens in red/white/blue;
toy chests of banana fiber from IKEA; desk from Pottery Barn; carpet from Karastan; flooring by Mohawk.
Child-friendly with aviation theme.

GIRL'S BEDROOM

CONCEPT

Vintage cast iron bed; vintage egg shape chair; custom blanket chest from Naula;
vintage dressers from client; desk from Pottery Barn; lamps with glass stems; carpet from Karastan;
flooring by Mohawk. Tween girl fashion theme with pinks, greens and oranges.

KITCHEN

CHAPTER | 4

A family with six children, extended family and friends—
along with significant entertaining—requires two kitchens: a
main kitchen and an overflow kitchenette in the basement.
The main kitchen space is the nexus point for family interaction,
and my team nicknamed this space the "hearth of the home."
Functionality and versatility were very important to ensure that
the space could handle entertaining and mealtimes, one of the
few scheduled times when this busy family can gather together.

We believe the kitchen space will become the central gathering
point within the home.

THE MAIN KITCHEN: *Hearth of the Home*

The primary design goal of the main kitchen was to create a "great room" effect with dimensions totaling 17 feet by 45 feet, with three interconnected spaces: a breakfast nook for casual meals or snacks, the kitchen prep space and a casual family living room space in which to congregate. This layout allows family members to interact prior to, during, and after their meals. The kitchens were designed down to the millimeter by Barbara Piazza of Euphoria Kitchens, with custom cabinetry from Holiday Kitchens. She used both CAD and hand drawings to ensure that the details were precise.

With the large island in the kitchen, meals can be served buffet style without interference in the preparation area. And adding a bar stool area to the island space allows more casual interaction for the family.

On the opposite side of the kitchen is the stove top with a prep area and a full-size refrigerator and full-size freezer on either side of the cooktop space.

On the west perimeter wall is the double-wall oven with a full wall of cabinetry that doubles as a butler's pantry. Within the island, flanking the sink, there are two dishwashers and a turbo microwave on the cooktop side. Near the breakfast nook, we placed a small bar sink and mini-refrigerator for quick snacks for the children during meal preparation.

On the north side of the 7-foot-wide island, there is a three-bin recycle center. Built to encourage active participation in keeping items out of the landfill, this idea was modeled on homes in Europe, which have recycling centers built into the kitchen. This three-drawer center was designed to allow the family to separate paper, plastics, bottles and standard rubbish.

LEFT: Kitchen from north to south.

ABOVE: Recycle bins.

At the opposite end of the kitchen, there is a space called the breakfast nook, which has a view of the south grounds. Our design team found a reclaimed 80-year-old Quaker pew while scouting for design products. Given that the family is quite religious, it seemed like a perfect touch to the "hearth of the home"—a spiritual touch in the kitchen.

We were thrilled when one of the friends of the family called and asked us to give them a suggestion for an item to purchase as a gift to the family. We suggested the pew and they were thrilled with the eco-friendly story of reusing a piece of furniture and saving it from the landfill. It is nice that the family will receive a unique gift from a dear friend! More casually, after the client saw the pew, they came up with the idea to place smaller tables in front so that it becomes a casual place to have a bit of breakfast or to read before starting the day. After school, the nook can transform into a cozy spot and healthy snack location. Given its southern light, it will be a great place to read a book too!

The bamboo flooring is also a highlight of the kitchen, given its naturally hypoallergenic properties. Says Ilene Lush of Chelsea Arts Tile & Stone, "We selected Dragonfly Bamboo for the flooring because they use mature species in their flooring which limits scratching and dents. Although we have many bamboo color options, we thought the caramelized color would be most similar to standard hardwood."

CUSTOM CABINETRY

The eco-friendly maple custom kitchen cabinetry around the perimeter of the kitchen is frameless, which is the newest trend in the United States, although common practice in Europe. Frameless construction uses 10 percent less wood and is eco-healthy because the cabinet interiors are more easily accessible for cleaning. And the Holiday Kitchens manufacturing process ensures that the paint and adhesives used are low-VOC. This is regulated by allowing the paint and adhesive to off-gas at the factory, and when the cabinets arrive, there is no chemical smell in the home.

The custom cabinetry is manufactured in the United States by Holiday Kitchens, a 64-year old U.S.-based firm that is a pioneer in the eco-friendly movement. After the Holiday team cuts the wood to minimize waste, the waste wood chunks become cutting boards; shavings become animal bedding; and sawdust is sold to be used for fire starter pellets.

The kitchen island uses framed custom cabinetry as this allows for more configuration options. And it supports an ECO by Cosentino countertop, which is one of the crowning achievements of the kitchen design. The product is sustainable and socially conscious and made of crushed materials such as porcelain sinks, glass, mirrors and other materials and is held together with a polymer based on corn resin. Certified by the cradle-to-cradle designation and other programs, this product is poised to be a game-changer in the eco-friendly movement—especially as people begin to recognize the finite resources of other natural materials. The island

and perimeter cabinetry is topped with the ECO material, and it appears to be a natural stone, but it is instead a product that has kept reusable materials from entering the landfill. Although it took a small bit of education and convincing for the client to be open-minded to this product, when they saw the installation, they were thrilled. At first people think that the countertop is granite, but then they view it more closely and ask "What is this?" after seeing the beauty of the countertop.

PREVIOUS PAGE: Vintage church pew; rough hewn tre water dispenser by ABC Home; breakfas tray and dishware by Fishs Eddy; floor by Dragonfly Bambo (CATS)

LEFT: Robert F. Kennedy Jr. in the new kitchen.

RIGHT: Electrolux appliances

APPLIANCES

We used Electrolux appliances in the Kennedy home due to the multiple options for kitchen and laundry appliances and HEPA vacuums. Says Electrolux, "We believe eco-friendly practices are important because we are striving to be a good neighbor in the communities in which we operate. After seeing the house, our immediate thought was how pleased we are to have a home that highlights the aesthetic beauty and versatility of the Electrolux appliances and showcases the benefits of incorporating 21st-century innovation with the latest in green technologies."

All appliances were Energy Star rated to ensure maximum efficiency. Most people know that the U.S. EPA created the Energy Star program as an energy efficiency rating system which ensures usage of 10-50 percent less energy than standard appliance models. This rating system helps businesses and individuals protect the environment.

Given that most average-sized homes spend close to $2,200 per year in energy bills, it was imperative that this 8,700 sf Kennedy home utilize as little energy as possible. The Electrolux team donated products to give consumers the awareness that energy efficient appliances do not have to compromise on design, functionality or quality. The firm has even taken steps to reduce energy consumption and emissions at its factories and to ensure that the functionality of these products allows a small (or large) meal or load of laundry to be done, while still reflecting the energy efficiency.

KITCHENETTE

The kitchenette is conveniently located downstairs, just off the media room and near the door to the outdoor pool. We installed stainless steel cabinets inset with glass panels. The backstory to the Carrara marble countertop is that it was found by the client and reclaimed from a Park Avenue demolition site. Recut to fit the space, this beautiful marble countertop provides a perfect contrast to the custom cabinetry, Kohler sink and faucet and Electrolux appliances. The kitchenette is the perfect place for preparing casual snacks, popcorn and drinks. Most important, when the kids and their friends are just out of the pool, they can run to the kitchenette (dripping wet onto the concrete floor!) rather than to the main kitchen upstairs.

And if the family is having a formal event, the kitchenette is a second place for caterers to wash dishes, store beverages or quickly reheat items. If anyone wants to raid the refrigerator late at night, they can easily hop on the elevator that goes from the private quarters to the basement and enjoy a movie in the media area just off the kitchenette.

Stainless steel kitchen by Holiday; reclaimed marble countertop; faucet by Kohler; microwave, refrigerator drawer and dishwasher by Electrolux; dishware by Fishs Eddy

DINING ROOM

Many families have a formal dining room that is off-limits except on special occasions. One of the wonderful discoveries in working with this client was learning that the family actually eats dinner together as many nights as possible. And they use their dining room! We had to design the space for usage on a regular basis, including protecting the floors from scratches by the chairs and using their existing table that was big enough to serve a minimum of ten people on a regular basis (parents, children, guests).

The dining room is accessed through a pocket door off the main kitchen or off the center hall. Both doors can be closed to separate the room from the kitchen or hallway if more privacy is needed.

The eco-friendly gas fireplace uses the latest technology to save energy (the pilot completely shuts off if the fireplace is not being used, thus preventing wasted energy) and ensures that the space has the ambience of a welcoming home— for either informal or formal gatherings.

Says Zach Tweardy of Majestic Fireplaces, "The fireplaces we installed are able to burn both wood and use gas. During my on-site consultation for the fireplace installation, we worked hard to remain compatible to the architects' vision, but we had to make a few modifications. The most important thing I learned is that the family embodies the ideals of conservation and it is not just lip service."

ENERGY STAR APPLIANCES

OPTION | 1

The U.S. Environmental Protection Agency (EPA) created the Energy Star program to qualify appliances that use 10-50% less water and electricity than standard models. They remind consumers that an appliance has two costs: the price paid at purchase and the cost for energy and water usage. A seal is granted to an appliance brand after extensive testing. This home used Electrolux appliances due to the high efficiency rating, cost efficiency and aesthetic beauty, plus other products such as HEPA-vacuums, which are perfect for a family with asthma, allergies and pets.

UNDER-CABINET LIGHTS

OPTION | 2

Low-profile under-cabinet lighting has become a more prevalent design option over the past two decades with options including xenon, LED or fluorescent. We do not recommend using low-voltage halogen bulbs as they have a short lifespan and generate heat. LED light bulbs last longest, do not generate heat and can be easily installed with new low-profile bars or flexible strips. Xenon lights have the most natural light and can be dimmed using standard ballasts. Fluorescent lights are the least expensive. We recommend LED lights.

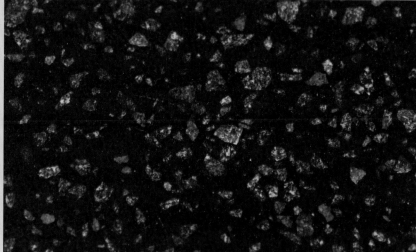

RECYCLE CENTER

OPTION | 3

The client designed a recycling center to facilitate a pattern of proper disposal of plastics, glass and paper. This is a more common practice in European homes, but it is becoming a new trend in the U.S. to have built-in bins within the island or under perimeter counters. With three bins on the kitchen island, the family will be easily able to sort items prior to disposal—and become trend leaders in this practice. Holiday Kitchens custom cabinetry allows any configuration in a kitchen layout.

COUNTERTOPS

OPTION | 4

There are so many options for counter-tops in the marketplace, including concrete, granite or bamboo. In this home, we specified the ECO by Cosentino product which is ground-breaking for the materials used during manufacture—crushed glass, mirrors, porcelain from sinks and fly ash from smokestacks—held together with a corn resin polymer to create an exceptionally durable countertop surface with multiple color options. Know that standard countertop height is 36 inches and standard bar height is 43 inches.

CABINETRY

OPTION | 5

The cabinetry was designed by Barbara Piazza of Euphoria Kitchens, who is a specialist in hand-drawing complicated kitchen spaces. She says, "A kitchen of this size with six children and two parents, plus guests, has to be designed for flexibility. Holiday Kitchens has both framed and frameless cabinet options—and over 90 door styles. This custom cabinetry line is both affordable and made with exceptional quality." And made in the U.S.A., this cabinetry is eco-friendly with low-VOC paints and stains, off-gasses at the factory and uses non-formaldehyde adhesives with minimal waste wood.

FURNITURE

OPTION | 6

We found an 80-year-old church pew that is perfect for the family breakfast nook. This nook is 17 feet wide, and using a reclaimed item with such a spiritual element is a nice addition to any home. Plus, we found bar stools that use reclaimed wood and were styled in a unique way to complement the linear elements of the kitchen. The kitchen furniture elements should always have non-formaldehyde-based glues to ensure that your indoor air quality is not contaminated.

DISHWARE

OPTION | 7

A family that entertains needs a significant amount of dishware. We used hotel-quality plates from Fishs Eddy when staging the home for photography. This dishware comes from hotels, or is manufactured anew using old methods for commercial dishware durability. The most important thing is that the dishware used for regular meals remain easy to clean and durable, to ensure that it does not end up in a landfill after a few uses. Simple white plates are the easiest way to go, and a hotel-quality plate will allow it to be washed and heated for many years without cracks in the glaze.

IMAGE COURTESY OF FISHS EDDY

FIXTURES

OPTION | 8

Faucets in the kitchen should have aerators to ensure that the water droplets feel bigger, leading to less water use than normal. The Kohler products used throughout the home are made of solid brass and zinc (not plastic) to ensure decades of use. The key to selecting any fixture in the kitchen is to ensure that the aesthetic beauty is complemented with superior innovation. And look for the WaterSense award designation (which is similar to the Energy Star program) to ensure that you have the most water-efficient product.

LIVING & WORKING

Home. Work. Study. Throughout the design process, the Kennedy family kept reminding our team that they are a family on the move. Despite their busy travel schedule, schools and related events, and charitable projects, the family maintains a family-centered home. Our focus was to understand that this is a home in constant transition, where everyone works, studies or prepares for travel. Any given day can start with Plan A but quickly transition to Plan K.

We tried to attempt a clutter-free environment, with a place for everything. And we tried to ensure that there are central gathering spaces for both informal and formal moments.

All the bookcases in the study, living and family rooms are lined with books, objects d'art and family heirlooms, yielding clues to the family's interests.

The family invited me over for Thanksgiving 2008 weekend to join them for dinner with a small group of friends. With perfect hosting and effortless energy, they simply let the evening evolve in an informal yet elegant manner. We began with pre-dinner political talks in the hallway off the formal living room, then moved into the dining room for dinner. After dinner, there was great laughter as the children gathered all of the candles in the house and lit them on a birthday cake—we thought the fire alarms would go off! Later we enjoyed dessert in the media room where we sat and watched a sporting event on television. A perfect evening with family and friends, and it showed me that we needed to design their home to allow the family to continue to build upon their traditions.

The newly redesigned formal living room includes multiple sofas, chairs, and a breakout seating area for private conversations. The piano, covered with a stuffed lizard, carved rhinoceros and family photographs, provides both a focal point and reminder that the family has a long history and interest in biodiversity. The taxidermy tiger was given to the Kennedy family many generations ago by an emperor, and although a bit moth-eaten, it is a treasured family heirloom.

The fireplace remains another anchor in the room, with a custom mantle designed by a wonderful Irish woodworker who looked at a photo and copied the design for all the mantles within a few weeks—simple elegance. With simply designed bookcases on either side of the fireplace, we were prepared to empty over forty boxes of books that are in storage, allowing these tomes to be easily accessed and enjoyed.

The flooring is the highlight in the formal living room—designed by carpentry impresario John Yarema, who, according to our client, "is the perpetual winner of various national annual 'Best Floor' awards." He took the reclaimed wood of two demolished antique homes in Baltimore, plus wood certified from the Forest Stewardship Council (FSC) and reclaimed wood from the old home to make this beautiful floor with an interlinked cylindrical pattern.

Additionally, the Yarema custom flooring is in the center hall, dining room, RFK study and the long upstairs hallway, which allows the family to pay homage to both the past and the present with the reclaimed wood in their new home.

ROBERT F. KENNEDY JR. STUDY

Designing the patriarch's study became a lesson in interpreting a simple exchange on a plane. The family invited me on a December 2008 trip to Deer Valley, Utah, for a charity event to benefit the Waterkeeper organization. While flying back to New York, I was seated next to Bobby, who was working on a speech or a book. Because he does not use a computer while traveling, he had stacks of papers, binders, and notebooks on the fold-down tray. He was working diligently and at some point, he looked up at the TV screen that I was watching and chuckled at my program choice—it was probably a home design show. At that moment, I took the headphones off and took the opportunity to ask him some questions about his future study space and his work habits.

RW: Do you use a laptop or desktop in your study?

RFK JR.: No, but I might start. I usually handwrite everything and then it is translated at the office.

RW: Do you plan to listen to music or watch TV when working in your office?

RFK JR.: No, I don't listen to music. Is that something that people do? [Chuckle] But a TV might be a good idea, so I can watch the news.

RW: Do you like certain colors?

RFK JR.: It doesn't matter. I just want a space for my stuff and want my home back.

After this exchange, there was little said for the rest of the trip as he got back to his writing. I jotted down a few notes with key words such as *home, low-tech, simple, non-intrusive, research* and began to contemplate what approach our team should take in designing his office.

The team of architects worked with the client to come up with the following ideas for Bobby's study: significant book storage, space for fossils and taxidermy, great light and peaceful energy to allow for productive thinking and writing. Our client was very clear on the vision, and clerestory windows became an absolutely vital part of the design to ensure that great light flowed into the space.

During our many design meetings, the use of millwork was quite extensive, and with the addition of a fireplace and clerestory windows to allow light

to penetrate the space throughout the day, we realized that with the addition of a rug, chairs, and a custom desk, the space would be complete. The flooring used in this space is the bit of reclaimed hardwood that was not mold-infested from the former home—thus serving as a link between the old and the new.

Heirlooms and priceless pieces were an important aspect to remember as part of the project, including the late Senator Robert F. Kennedy's desk. We used his father's desk in the study, but due to their height difference (the desk was made for a man of 5'8" and Bobby is 6'2"), it will be placed in the private quarters at a later date. This location allows for contemplative viewing but with limited traffic. Private family mementos will remain on the desk.

Sofa and chairs by Mitchell Gold + Bob Willams; reclaimed steel table by ABC Home; lamps, small table and accessories by Housing Works; Crestron panel; throws by Melange Home; steel disc bowl by The Nest Store; bookcase items from client; carpets by Karastan.

FAMILY ROOM

As we mentioned in the kitchen chapter, our design meetings continued to emphasize the informal living room off the kitchen. My design terminology suggests that this room is an extension of the "hearth of the home," specifically for the more intimate group of friends and family who will naturally gravitate to the casual space off the kitchen. There, people find comfortable seating, pillows and lamps to encourage reading books or relaxing in front of the flat-panel TV. The flooring in this space is a continuation of the sustainably harvested bamboo used in the kitchen.

One of the design signatures throughout the home is pocket doors. For example, in this casual living room space off the kitchen, the doors will remain open most of the time, using pocket doors to allow the room to "disappear." At other rare times, the space can become private as needed.

When the children come in from school and enter this living space, it will allow a watchful parental eye during family meal preparation, homework completion, television viewing or videogame activities. We hope this space will also be a contemplative location for reading a book, planning an event menu or an informal space to meet with friends.

> "[Green design] . . . is more than a trend. It's a complete shift in human consciousness that is going to trigger so much innovation in design."
>
> PAULETTE COLE
> *CEO, ABC Home*

CHILDREN'S DESKS

With school and work needs in mind, we made sure the children's bedrooms were outfitted with a desk. The children are quite smart and use computers for most of their assignments. We ensured that there is a place for pencils and that recycled paper tablets are ready for homework assignments, note taking, or analyzing information from Internet searches. Two of the desks in the children's rooms are reclaimed—we found them as they were about to be discarded from a business office and dumped into the landfill.

In another bedroom, the desk was custom installed by Easy Closets, which is LEED-friendly due to its factory being within a 500-mile radius of the project site.

LEFT: Custom installed desk by Easy Closets.

RIGHT: Reclaimed desk that was saved from landfill.

SLEEPING

CHAPTER 6

One-third of our lives are spent sleeping, which is why the bedroom is a great place to start when designing an eco-healthy home. After the home was infested with black mold, the Kennedy children began to suffer from asthma, allergies and pneumonia. They were especially prone to wheezing and sneezing in the evening, which necessitated preventative measures such as nebulizers and air purifiers.

One of the basic management tools in a space is to ensure that a multitude of potential irritants—dust, dust mites and triggers—are eliminated or managed. For example, we found that the Somnium mattresses used throughout the home do not have toxic chemicals or off-gassing, which eliminates potential triggers for an allergic or asthmatic person. And we always recommend using hypoallergenic covers for the pillows and mattresses.

GUEST ROOM

The client wanted the guest room to be sophisticated and elegant and to feel like a secret hideaway. The amenities provided for guests were inspired by an amalgam of travel locations, including yoga retreats, spas and estates. The room is spacious, and due to the foliage outside the windows, remains darkened until mid-morning to ensure a longer sleep. Additionally, the space is more relaxing with simple touches such as the upholstered headboard, organic linens, a writing desk and an ever-changing mélange of books. The blanket chest at the foot of the bed ensures that a guest can take any extra pillows and blankets without having to search for them.

Given that two of the adult children are in college, the client wanted to make sure that they had private space if they decide to have a lengthy stay. With direct access from the side entrance, this space allows an easier entry without disturbing the family, so a guest will not feel intrusive, but will be able to maintain a different schedule from the family if needed.

The bathroom is spacious, and all the products and amenities are in place so that one does not have to search for items. So, forgetting something is not a problem—there is always a little sample size waiting for you!

In addition, we had a custom closet designed to ensure maximum storage with drawers, a hamper and a luggage rack provided. This will hopefully encourage a guest to unpack their bags versus living out of the suitcase for the duration of their stay.

Grey flannel organic cotton bedding; vintage headboard, tables and blanket chest from client; carpets by Karastan.

MASTER BEDROOM

The master bedroom suite has exposure on the north, south and west sides, so it has a limited need for lighting during the day. The windows provide an expansive view of the grounds which allows the parents to observe the children without leaving the room. When the foliage clears, this allows them to see a small perimeter of the lake in the winter and the outbuildings at the rear of the property, including the garage.

The east wall has a fireplace, and it will be a place where they can read a book, rest and warm their feet by the fire while viewing the property. With the wide-plank, Mohawk-engineered flooring, atop a radiant floor, the room remains cozy.

The bed has a Somnium eco-mattress, and with an abundance of hypoallergenic pillows and organic sheets, this will allow a perfect night's sleep.

RIGHT: Upholstered chairs by Mitchell Gold + Bob Williams; accessories by Vivaterra, Housing Works and The Nest Store; carpet by Karastan; artwork by client.

OPPOSITE: Uphol-stered headboard and chair by Mitchell Gold + Bob Williams; vintage side tables and lamps by client; organic cotton linens by Melange Home/ Laytner's Linens; carpet by Karastan.

OPPOSITE: Organic cotton linens; tent and banana fiber chests by IKEA; accessories by ABC Home and Housing Works; bike from ABC Home; carpet by Karastan; floor by Mohawk.

BOY'S ROOM

The youngest child was most affected by the toxic black mold in the old house. We took particular care to locate a HEPA air purifier in this room, only a few yards from the head of the bed. It is a larger unit that is approximately two feet tall and emits white noise that helps with relaxation should a bout with wheezing and sneezing occur. Many clients forget that they should change the filters of these air purifiers, so we recommend that you add it to your calendar to ensure that you don't aggravate a respiratory problem by forgetting to clean them.

Some scientists argue that these air purifiers don't work, but the jury is out—and for most parents, they will take every measure to attempt to find a solution that works for their child. Other measures were taken, such as cleaning the rugs and using hypoallergenic pillows and covers to ensure that

dust mites are kept to a minimum. There are no window drapes in this room, although if they were installed, we would only install shades or shutters that can be cleaned simply by vacuuming.

Since he regularly has sleepovers, we designed the room to feature twin beds, which is perfect for sleepovers. We obtained twin beds made from recycled barnwood timbers from Vermont, which is also within the 500-mile radius to allow additional carbon points.

The whimsical motif of blue walls and a tent with toys represents a common area of interest for a typical boy under the age of ten. But the closet area has the most fascination for him, due to the Solatube, which allows passive light to come into the space.

GIRL'S ROOM

The youngest daughter's room was designed with a Mod theme, reflecting her interest in fashion and photography. The pink walls were selected by the client—and we designed the concept with vintage black-and-white fashion photos, which are perfect for a tween, as her interests may change. When we did the photos, we decided to leave the walls blank to showcase the low-VOC paints.

The focal point of the room is the retro-vintage Egg chair in the corner in which she can curl up to read a book or do fashion sketches. The chair is covered with an wool fabric and is fashionable. The rest of the furniture is heirloom furniture, with the exception of the reclaimed desk.

OPPOSITE: Organic cotton linens; Somnium mattress; blanket chest by Naula and throw by Laytner's Linens.

TOP LEFT: Retro chair by Bo Concept; Recycled flip-flop basket.

LEFT: Tween accessories.

LINENS

Our short list of design options required organic linens, hypoallergenic pillows and pillow/mattress covers that could be washed regularly. For the textiles, we used hypoallergenic organic cotton linens and pillows instead of feather pillows; some people are sensitive to the dander in the feathers.

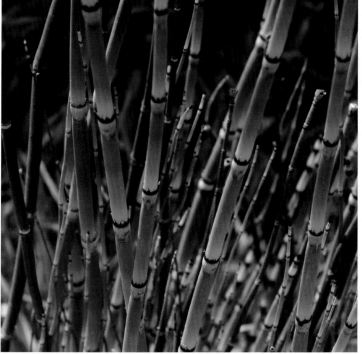

ECO-FRIENDLY TEXTILE OPTIONS

●

ORGANIC COTTON

SILK

CORN FIBER

BAMBOO FIBER

RECYCLED COTTON

SOY FIBER*

●

Research the manufacturing process to ensure a non-formaldehyde soaked product.

With dust comes our ugly friend the microscopic dust mite, which feeds on the cells of our skin. These microscopic creatures are found in bedding, carpeting and under beds. The carcass of a dust mite is the trigger for allergic individuals. Because female dust mites lay up to a hundred eggs per month, you can imagine a lot of potential wheezing and sneezing.

Off-gassing is caused when mattresses have petroleum-based chemicals inside the fiber of the mattress—chemicals such as antimony (arsenic), boric acid (roach killer), deca (flame retardant) and formaldehyde (carcinogen), which is sometimes used in an adhesive to hold mattresses together. These chemicals "off-gas" vapors that are called volatile organic compounds (VOCs). These vapors, for those who are sensitive, can cause respiratory problems and skin irritation and have been linked to asthma, allergies and lung, nose and throat cancers.

We found an eco-healthy mattress company that would work with people with chemical sensitivities. The patented Somnium eco-friendly foam mattress was the best option, especially because it does not off-gas, and because they were developed by a former gymnast who had back problems. A design with proper back and side support ensures perfect sleeping posture, thus allowing for a more restful sleep.

> "Our product is the next generation of spring mattresses with hypoallergenic properties."
>
> SUSANNE FLOTHER
> *Somnium*

Our client insisted on no window drapes, since they are dust catchers. Since the family lives on acreage with a perimeter of forest-land, they are able to go without window shades, unlike most homes with neighbors that are in close proximity. The home will eventually have some rooms outfitted with window shutters or shades, but the only immediate priority is in spaces requiring privacy, such as bathrooms.

FLOORING

For a family with asthma and allergies, we recommend hardwood flooring with rugs that can be washed or aired regularly. The Karastan rugs are made of recycled nylon fibers, wool, or sisal and are typically hypoallergenic. Most people do not think about their flooring, but it is the largest dust collector in a home. In addition to the custom flooring in the rest of the home, all the bedrooms were covered with Mohawk-engineered hardwood flooring, which is recommended for use with radiant heat as it does not expand and contract like standard hardwood. Learn more in Chapter 12.

NOISE & LIGHT POLLUTION

An eco-healthy home must also deal with one of the most hidden elements: noise pollution—an often overlooked reason for poor sleep patterns. Studies have shown that the optimal amount of sleep for most people is between six to eight hours, without interruption. Since the house is located on a well-trafficked roadway, all bedroom walls were reinforced with extra insulation to limit what is called "noise-carry" between rooms, and double-paned windows with UV glass were selected for both noise reduction and energy efficiency.

FURNITURE

OPTION | 1

Bargain basement or discount furniture with formaldehyde adhesives is not a deal—as items could have cancer-causing chemicals that off-gas into your sleeping environment. Homeowners should visit stores who screen vendors to ensure that they use eco-friendly and sustainable practices from harvesting wood, non-toxic glues and low-VOC paints and stains. Ask the questions before bringing your bed home. Please make sure to review the furniture for your baby nursery to ensure your child is sleeping in an eco-healthy crib!

MATTRESS

OPTION | 2

Given that we spend 70% of our lives sleeping, it is important to know that you are not breathing in carcinogens that are commonly added to mattresses. Mattresses that off-gas produce a chemical smell and are often toxic. It is best to investigate eco-foam or non-toxic options with strong back support to ensure a good night sleep. Also, make sure to cover the mattress with a washable mattress cover. Says Rainer Wieland of Somnium, "Your posture is the key to a better quality of life, and your mattress can significantly influence your body alignment." The Kennedy Home only uses Somnium mattresses and foundations.

IMAGE COURTESY OF SOMNIUM

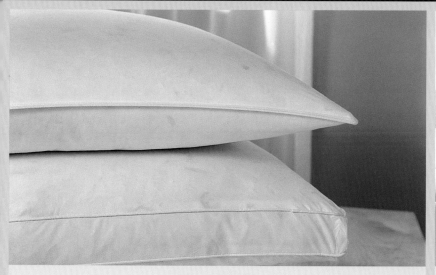

PILLOWS

OPTION | 3

Hypoallergenic, buckwheat, foam and down pillows are all options to consider as long as you use a washable pillow cover. All pillows should have a hypoallergenic pillow cover that can be washed regularly to ensure your pillows do not become infested with dust mites. Make sure to wash your pillows and to replace them regularly. We did an informal survey and found that most people have a pillow that is over three years old, which is not washed on a regular basis. Many people experience an immediate improvement in quality of sleep when pillows are replaced.

SHEETS

OPTION | 4

Organic cotton, silk, fleece and bamboo are the most common sheets used today. Since we spend a significant portion of our lives in bed, it is important to recognize the impact a better quality sheet may have on your long-term health. The difference between regular and organic cotton is the use of pesticides—and the less you are exposed to, the better your health. We recommend buying the best sheets you can afford.

IMAGE COURTESY OF LAYTNER'S LINEN & HOME

IMAGE COURTESY OF LAYTNER'S LINEN & HOME

FLOORS

OPTION | 5

Floor spaces are the largest dust collectors in a home, and dust mites are the enemy when designing an eco-healthy home environment. It is not recommended that wall-to-wall carpet be used, but rugs or carpet tiles over a floor can allow better indoor air quality. A rug or carpet tile can be washed or aired out to maintain good indoor air quality. Regular mopping, dusting and vacuuming with a HEPA-filter vacuum can be helpful.

WINDOW TREATMENTS

OPTION | 6

One issue most people ignore when trying to get a good night sleep is light pollution. A well-fitted set of blinds, shades or shutters is a great choice. The circadian rhythms for most people are disrupted, and it is a good idea to ensure blackout shades are in place to ensure a full night of sleep. Drapes are rarely used in the bedroom of an asthmatic because they are simply dust catchers. The most important thing in your sleeping environment is the ability to clean window treatments regularly to ensure an eco-healthy environment.

IMAGE COURTESY OF HUNTER DOUGLAS

STUFFED ANIMALS

OPTION | 7

Children with asthma must beware of triggers such as their favorite stuffed animal, which often acts like a petri dish for dust mites, which can causing a moment of wheezing and sneezing during the night. Most parents use the following methods to keep the sleeping area eco-healthy: wash the animal at least once a month inside a pillow case to limit wear and tear, and after the animal has dried, pop it into a freezer bag overnight. The freezer process will ensure that any mites that survive are frozen and will fall into the bottom of the bag.

AIR PURIFIER

OPTION | 8

Bedrooms require good indoor air quality and many families with asthma and allergy issues use air filtration devices, especially as they can improve a wheezing and sneezing situation. The white noise from the machines can also assist those who are light sleepers. The Austin Air Purifier has the best overall air protection for those with allergies and asthma—with three filters to remove dust, pollen, dander, mold, mold spores and odors. One of the biggest issues for these machines is energy usage, so make sure to turn them off when not occupying the space.

IMAGE COURTESY OF ABC CARPET & HOME

BATHING

CHAPTER 7

One of the most humorous and challenging moments for every parent has to be the nightly bath-time ritual and early morning rush as everyone is getting ready for school. Another item on the Kennedy family wish list was ensuring that all bedrooms had a private bathroom *en suite* to avoid a "take-a-number" rush each morning. With the exception of the powder room and bath spa in the basement, everyone has their own private bathroom space.

In each bathroom, we used Kohler products which are rated by the U.S. EPA WaterSense program (similar to the Energy Star program for appliances) with a focus on water efficiency. This program has been around for a few years, and the products used in the home illustrate the beautiful options available. For example, we installed 1.6-gallon-per-flush toilets in most of the bathrooms, but we also installed dual-flush toilets that use even less water on a small flush. Also, the low-flow faucets and the showerheads throughout the home utilize aerators to make water droplets feel bigger, so less water is used when washing hands or bathing. What is quite exciting is that Kohler does not charge extra fees for the eco-friendly bathroom fixture option, which typically requires more research and development.

Eco-friendly measures continue with the textiles—through the use of organic cotton or bamboo for towels, rugs, shower curtains and robes. Most importantly, we only recommend the use of nylon shower liners (no vinyl!) to prevent off-gassing—or glass dividers, which are even better, as the glass can be recycled at the end of its usage.

PREVIOUS PAGE: Hat-box toilet by Kohler.

LEFT, ABOVE & OPPOSITE: Child's bathroom with Kohler fixtures; tile by Dal-Tile; towels by Laytner's Linens; engineered wood floors by Mohawk flooring.

MASTER BATH

The master bathroom was designed to allow ease of use for two people in a single area. However, we did not create a mega-bath, which is a trend we often see in suburban homes. Rather, this is a room that is a bit larger than a standard size bath, containing a stand-alone jetted tub and separate walk-in shower and water closet—all of which allow for maximum privacy in a smaller space.

Another amenity that was installed is a towel warmer—we were able to locate a corner to install this in the master bathroom—a simple amenity which can provide additional comfort during the winter months.

Our favorite millworker built a custom seven-foot bath vanity with "his & her" washbasins based on a client drawing. This vanity allows undermount sinks, which is another opportunity to ensure that cleanliness is maintained. The bathroom flooring contains radiant heat, which allows our client to stand with bare feet on a tiled floor on the coldest day, even in the cold winters in the Northeast.

In addition, we utilized a new surface for the entire bathroom (floors, shower walls, tub surround) called ECO by Cosentino, which is an eco-product containing crushed materials such as mirrors, porcelain (from toilets/sinks), glass, cups and fly ash from smokestacks—all held together by a corn resin polymer. All these substances would typically enter a landfill, and this surface highlights a way to bring beauty to your space with an eco-friendly product. This ECO product can be used for both kitchen countertops and bathrooms, on walls and floor surfaces.

All bathrooms are also equipped with non-toxic soaps, cleaners and no-dye recycled toilet paper.

LEFT: Master bath
with view of water
closet in background.

BATH SPA

Even though the new home will not have the same toxic black mold issues, the long-term side effects of their exposure to the mold at a young age has become an issue for the children. Most parents who have children with asthma and allergies remember taking their child into the bathroom in the middle of the night to steam up the shower.

The wish list for the new home included a sauna and steam shower in the bath spa in the basement level. The entire spa is a wet room with Dal-Tile on the floor, ECO tile on the walls and a central drain. This allows the entire room to be "wet," which is a great idea for an area off the pool. The pre-built sauna unit by Mr. Steam uses 220 volts of electricity for light and power, while the adjacent steam shower has a small unit the size of a large shoe box, which uses less than two gallons of water for a standard twenty-minute steam.

Since this area is also used as a changing room for those using the pool, it is outfitted with hooks on the wall and a makeup/dressing table with small chairs. Just outside the space, there are six red Bisley lockers made of reclaimed steel, which can be used for storing clothing while the guests are swimming.

FIXTURES

OPTION | 1

The most important thing to remember when selecting bath fixtures is to focus on low-flow options for water efficiency. In the past, most showers used 5 to 8 gallons per minute, but more recently, they use between 1.6 to 2.5 gallons per minute. Ensure that you look for an aerator in the faucet, which allows the water droplets to feel larger, encouraging less water use during a shower. Most people don't realize that in a five-minute shower, they can consume up to 40 gallons of water—make sure you use a low-flow option that can save up to 12 gallons per shower!

TOILETS

OPTION | 2

Kohler products were used in the home because of the many options—from a very stylish Hatbox toilet to a modern square toilet to a dual-flush (1.4 to 1.6 gallons) option. Many of the toilets have a feature called power-assist to ensure a solid flush with minimal spray for an eco-healthy bathroom. One of the exciting thing about the Kohler water-efficient products is that there is no price differentiation for selecting an eco-friendly choice. And with water efficiency leadership for consecutive years since 2008 as recipient of the WaterSense awards, Kohler is committed to continued research and new innovation.

SHOWER CURTAIN

OPTION | 3

Many people recognize the chemical smell when opening a new vinyl shower curtain liner. The smell is due to the off-gassing of the pliable plastics. To be eco-friendly, it is highly recommended that you only use nylon shower curtain liners, with a cotton exterior curtain. There is no off-gassing and it is hypo-allergenic and mildew resistant. Additionally, exterior curtains often come in organic cotton, bamboo or other silk, which is always a better alternative than vinyl. The cost is quite similar, but it is priceless for your health.

TILE AND STONE

OPTION | 4

Tile and stone release few VOCs after installation and the grout has cured. Those with asthma and allergies are able to tolerate these surfaces better, and they can also be sealed, thus reducing the propensity for mold and mildew in a wet area. A big positive is the fact that with proper maintenance, these materials will last more than fifty years. We used Dal-Tile (ceramic, porcelain and glass), plus reclaimed tile throughout the home. There are so many eco-options in the market that one should allow plenty of time to review.

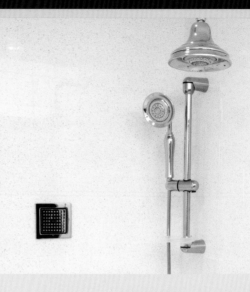

LIGHTING

OPTION | 5

Bathroom lighting requires more thought than most people think—a single ceiling fixture will create shadows. Lighting in layers is the best solution: mirror, shower, water closet and tub area lights will ensure that the mood is appropriate. And it is also nice to place dimmers on the lights if you want to turn your bath into a spa moment. The perfect level for a wall sconce on either side of the mirror is 66 inches from the finished floor to limit shadows while shaving or applying makeup.

STEAM SHOWER

OPTION | 6

We specified a Mr. Steam unit for the steam shower in the master bath and the spa. This steam shower product has been specified by designers and architects for over fifty years, and remains one of the most water-efficient products, utilizing less than two gallons per steam. A family with asthma and allergies can benefit from the use of a steam shower as there may be a therapeutic value for wellness—improving breathing and muscle tightness.

TEXTILES

OPTION | 7

Organic or recycled cotton is the way to go; most people do not realize that cotton is the most heavily pesticided plant in the world. Using organic cotton towels, robes, rugs and shower curtains is a way to ensure that you are not lowering your indoor air quality. According to Laytner's Linens, "Bathroom textiles have a wide array of colors, patterns and textures. Buy the best you can afford. Good quality options will ensure that you are not disposing of defective towels into a landfill." On a cost-per-use basis, an organic cotton or recycled cotton product is a great value.

CLEANERS

OPTION | 8

We recommend the very affordable Method cleaning products, which contain the word "natural" on the label meaning all the ingredients are natural. The soaps do not contain parabens, triclosan or animal products (cleaners are considered vegan) and phtalates are not included in packaging. All products are reviewed by a team of scientists to ensure that the final products are biodegradable, non-toxic and safe for marine life. Like so many products on the market, they are not organic, but are considered eco-friendly.

IMAGE COURTESY OF METHOD

STORAGE

One needs little imagination to picture the trail of items children leave behind in multiple locations from the moment of entering a home. After observation and discussion, we designed landing spots and storage locations to guarantee that everything—whether visible on a table or hiding in a cupboard or closet—has its place (even if it doesn't end up there!) with ease of access.

From the mudroom to the luggage closet to the linen closet, the storage options are extensive.

OPPOSITE & ABOVE:
Mudroom with
EasyClosets cubbies
and durable cobble-
block floors allows
easy landing spot
when children come
into home.

KEEP TOXINS OUTSIDE

Any LEED-certified home accumulate points if there is a method used at all entry points to ensure external dirt and toxins remain outside the home rather than entering the main living space.

In this home, there are several entry points—the main entrance, the garage and service entrances, plus the basement loggia area. Each space was designed so that when guests enter, there is a place for visitors to sit as they remove their shoes before placing them in a basket or cubby. In the vestibule outside the main front door, there is a bench, and in the mudroom off the garage, there are cubbies for coats, boots and shoes.

We used the EasyClosets storage system in the mudroom to allow a custom solution at an affordable price.

BEDROOM CLOSETS

To facilitate ease of dressing, each closet was outfitted with EasyClosets, a custom closets firm that designed them with shaker panels and built-in hampers. The closets have built-in drawers and double-hang rods, allowing for an easy match of pants or skirts with shirts and blouses. The adjustable shelving allows easy access to sweaters or T-shirts, depending on the season. The installation was done in two days and the manufacturing process took less than two weeks!

The master bedroom closets have special features including tie racks, pant racks, shoe racks and dry-cleaning rods. When we were working with the closet design team, we reviewed two important factors: our client's day-to-day routine and whether the client was a right-handed or a left-handed. Each of these factors can assist in determining where to place the key elements that people reach for each day, such as watches, cufflinks, socks and scarves.

Also, Solatube devices were installed in each closet, allowing daily passive lighting in the space and eliminating the need to use electrical lighting during the day, saving energy and lowering electricity usage. Learn more in Chapter 13.

OPPOSITE: His closet with a bamboo charging tower for phones and PDAs to limit phantom power usage.

TOP LEFT & BOTTOM LEFT: Double hang to maximize storage; drycleaning/dressing rod to allow a neat closet prep space.

OPPOSITE: The west wall of the kitchen has ample storage in a wall of cabinetry.

TOP LEFT: Cabinets contain pull-out drawers.

TOP RIGHT: Appliance garage stores seldom used appliances.

KITCHEN STORAGE

Preparing meals and entertaining in the main kitchen (or the "hearth of the home") requires meticulous planning and organization for a family with six children. The family maintains an organic diet for regular meals, with exceptions made for sleepovers and entertaining guests.

In the quest to ensure proper storage, our client makes it a practice to label everything, including the contents of each drawer, shelf and pantry section. The pantry wall of custom cabinetry in the main kitchen allows storage of dishes, glassware and serving platters, as well as non-perishable food, thus making everything centralized and easier to access when preparing meals and entertaining.

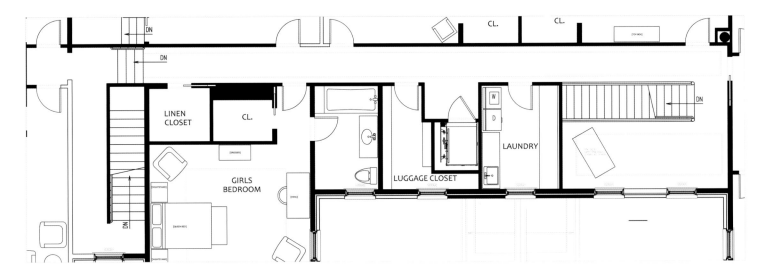

BASIC STORAGE

After observing the family as they prepared for a trip, we decided to locate a luggage room on the second level, near the elevator. This allows the family to pack for a trip without getting luggage from the basement, and then trudging upstairs, and then bringing it back downstairs. Having the luggage room in the private quarters will also ensure that there is a place for everything when there is a quick getaway.

In another section of the basement, there is an open-format storage room that will contain wire shelves to be used for overflow storage items and can be used as an extension of the bulk storage from the pantry.

Also, the outdoor loggia space has an exterior pool storage area so that wet pool items will not be brought into the home.

ABOVE: Floorplan for 2nd floor with laundry, luggage and linen closets.

OPPOSITE: A place for everything; (counterclockwise) laundry room, closet drawers, linen closet and mudroom cubby. Paperstone countertop in laundry room.

CLEANING

CHAPTER 9

Indoor air quality is one of the most important concerns when creating an eco-healthy home. In fact, many people are just learning that indoor air quality can be ten times worse than outdoor air quality because of the mixture of off-gassing from furniture, mattresses and cleaning chemicals mixed and re-circulated into the air. Simple things can be done to prevent this and the simplest among them is to ensure that your furnishings do not add toxins to your living space, which can further lower indoor air quality.

For example, non-toxic cleansers do not contain a high percentage of toxic chemicals. Oftentimes, standard cleaners have artificial scents that overpower a room with a pine or chemical smell, which has led many consumers to equate this scent with cleanliness. A cleanser that is non-toxic will state so clearly on the label, and often will use herbal scents instead of synthetic chemicals. When cleaning, make sure to use fresh sponges so that you are not spreading around mold or E. coli when attempting to clean your space. LEED practices encourage homeowners to pay close attention to the management of dust, allergen triggers and toxins.

BEDROOM

Bed linens should be washed in warm or hot water at least once a week.

Upholstery on your couches and chairs can harbor more than dust mites. E. coli can also be present, especially if your pets jump onto the furniture after using a litter box or relieving themselves outdoors.

Upholstery on couches and chairs is a territory that often hides dust mites. Thus it is important to clean pillows and slipcovers on a regular basis.

The best flooring solution in a bedroom is hardwood floors with rugs that can be aired out on a regular basis, instead of wall-to-wall carpeting.

Make sure to review feather pillows and feather filling within your bedding or couches. If you are wheezing or sneezing whenever you enter a room, you could be allergic to the fill.

When people change or wash their pillow, allergies or sleep issues often clear up quickly. Wash your pillow at least every six to twelve months and use a zippered pillow cover that is regularly washed. Most people will keep a pillow for years, but if they were to have their pillow tested, they would be shocked to find microbes, dust mites and other bacteria living within the cover.

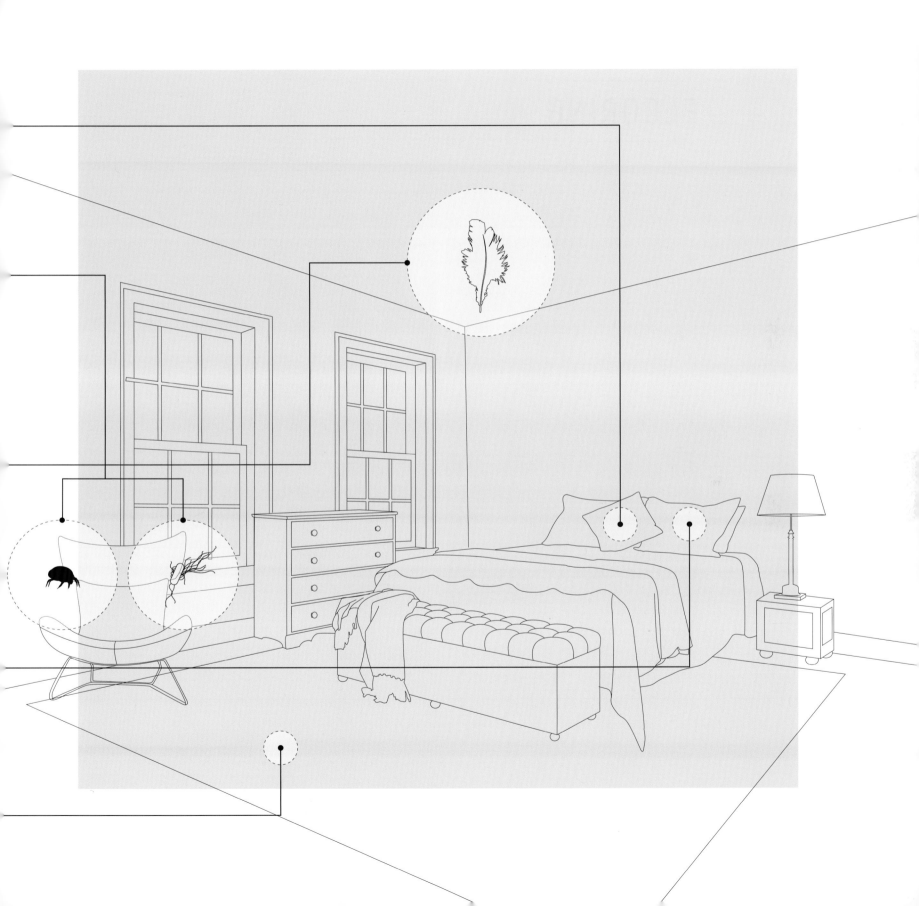

FLOORING

Flooring is the biggest surface that catches dust.

Cleansers used on hardwood floors should not contain petrochemicals that will affect the indoor air quality.

Hardwood flooring should be cleaned with a minimally damp mop or electrostatic mop to ensure dust removal.

Consider staining floors with tung oil, which is wallet-friendly because only a minimal amount is needed. It provides a tough, water-resistant finish with a golden hue that does not darken noticeably with age.

Carpets should be cleaned routinely and rugs should be aired regularly to lower the prevalence of dust or dust mites.

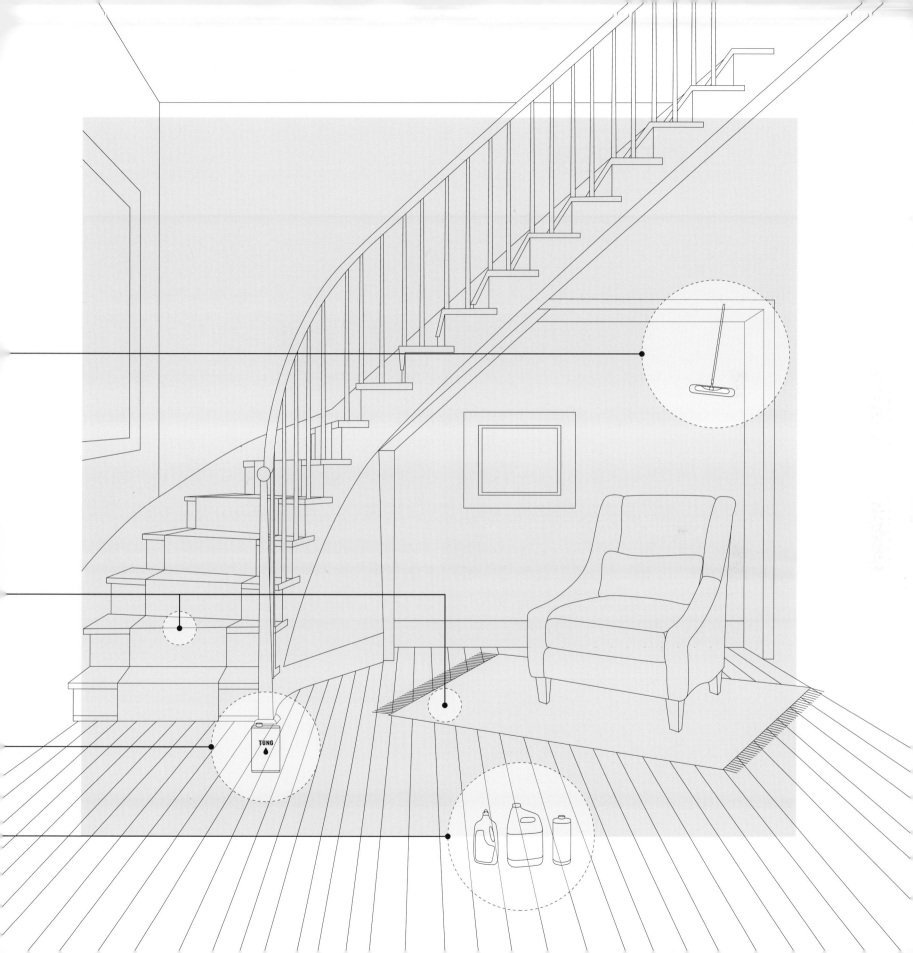

KITCHEN

The kitchen is a space that people overlook by focusing only on the cleanliness of countertops and sinks.

Cabinetry with frames is often a culprit for hidden dirt, dust and vermin.

The filter for a hood over a range with a cooktop should be changed periodically.

The filter for your refrigerator water and ice maker should be changed every six to twelve months to prevent bacteria.

Mold can grow in the refrigerator pan if the water is not emptied on a regular basis.

When you go on vacation, do not leave a load of dishes in the machine dishwasher with the heat cycle on, or when you come back, you will probably be eating off of moldy plates.

A freestanding stove should be pulled out on an annual basis to clean up crumbs and other detritus that fall behind it.

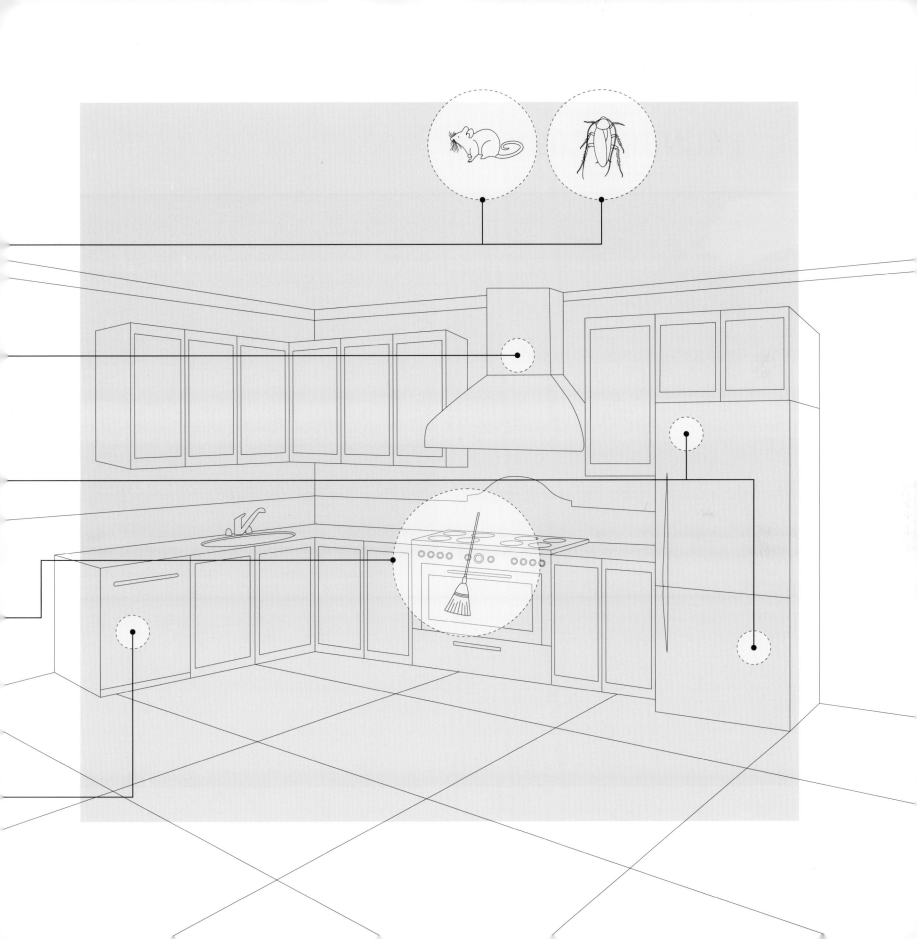

LAUNDRY ROOM

Concentrated detergents mean you will dispose of less packaging.

Lint traps for dryers should be cleaned with each load, and the exterior vent should be cleaned regularly to ensure that there is no fire hazard.

Detergents should be low in phosphorus; otherwise, waterways can be polluted by runoff, encouraging algae overgrowth.

Front-load washers should be cleaned regularly using a mixture of one part vinegar or bleach to one part water.

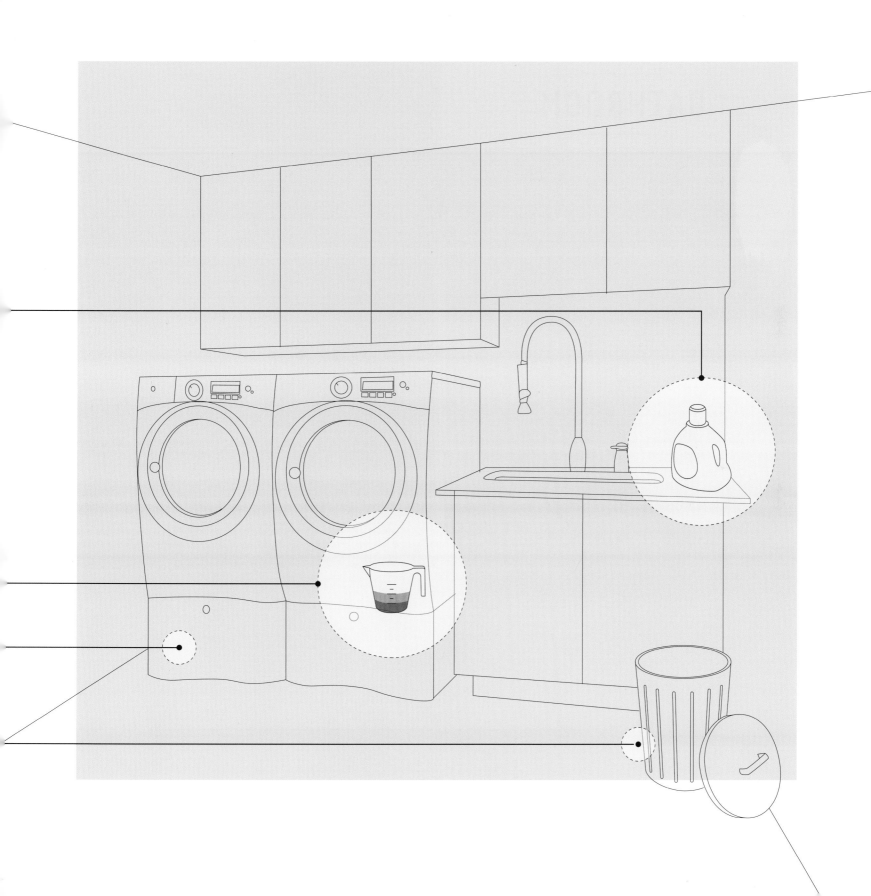

BATHROOM

Use recycled or non-dyed toilet paper.

Always flush the toilet with a closed lid and ensure that toothbrushes and facecloths are placed far away from the toilet.

Always use a nylon shower curtain liner.

Replace your shower curtain when you see mold buildup.

Always flush the toilet with a closed lid.

Try to design a separate water-closet space from the rest of the bathroom.

Ensure your cleansers are labeled non-toxic.

Regularly replace your sponges used for cleaning.

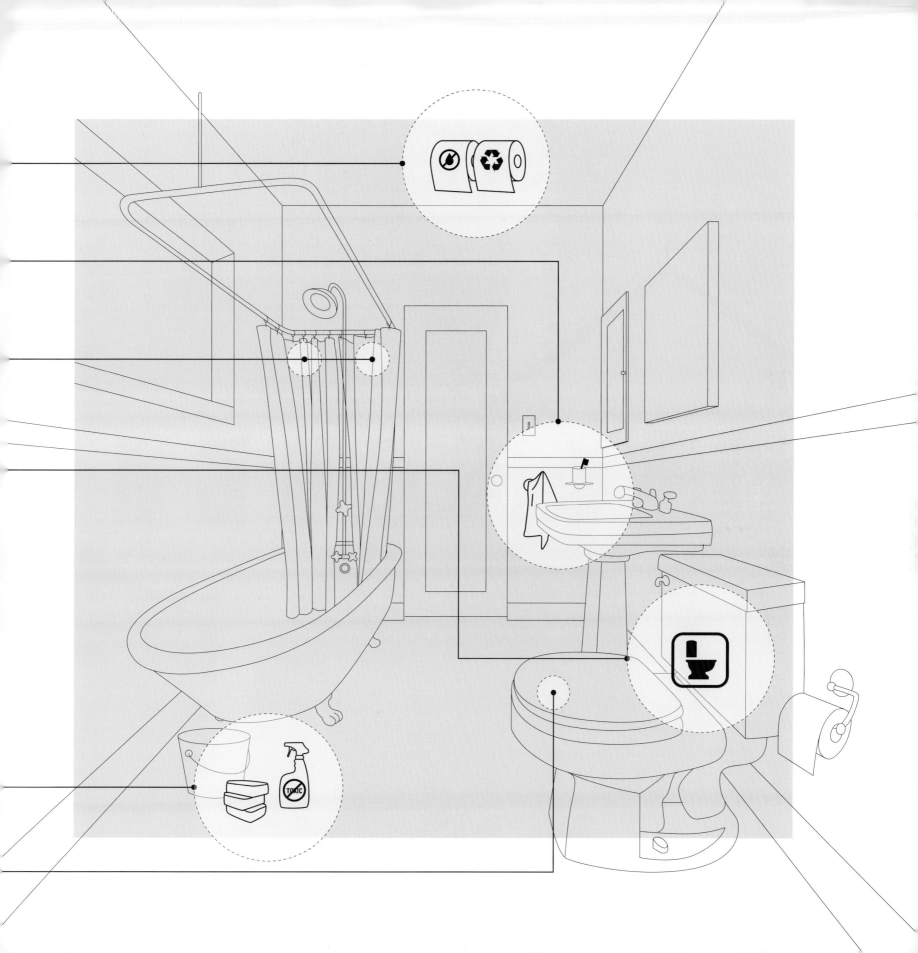

OUTDOORS

For the Kennedy family, relaxation is sometimes difficult to find given their hectic schedules for work, school, travel and other commitments. The home sits on twelve acres of land facing a thirty-acre private lake, and the freedom to play, climb trees, create adventures, swim, and find contemplative spaces for privacy in the forest or the outbuildings will ensure many family memories. The architects' goal was to create outdoor spaces to encourage moments of clarity and rest whenever possible.

The interior of the home on the main level is adjacent to a wraparound terrace with a view of the grounds and the pool space. From the center hall, the study or the formal living room, family and guests can walk through the French doors to enjoy an *al fresco* drink or dinner. The terrace features a mélange of eco-friendly items, such as the aluminum railing, reclaimed bluestone tile, and rocks from the property used to construct the terrace wall.

On the lower level, there is a loggia, an informal covered space off the media room which overlooks the pool. This is a shaded breezeway that keeps the space cool even on the hottest days and is an alternative location for cookouts during inclement weather. In the middle of the summer, it will offer a cool spot to sit while monitoring activity in the pool area. The exterior walls feature exposed stone on the exterior of the home which came from the traditional method of chiseling rocks from the property. As an ideal spot for private conversations, the loggia will be a cool refuge on a hot day—and is sure to become a spot for friends and neighbors gathering to enjoy the pool, cookouts, falconry and fishing.

The exterior railing is black aluminum which resembles wrought iron, but it is easily recycled at the end of its usage. Easy to maintain and non-rusting, this is a product that is one-third the price of wrought iron and surrounds the external terrace.

MULTI-GENERATIONAL DESIGN

CHAPTER | 11

The Kennedy family has been a leading proponent of legislation for accessibility in public and private spaces since the introduction of the pioneering Americans with Disabilities Act (ADA), spearheaded through Congress by the late Senator Edward Kennedy and signed into law in July 1990.

So many families focus on childproofing their homes without thinking about the various stages of life. On this project, we also had an opportunity to address a little-discussed principle called universal, or multi-generational, design. Our client indicated a wish to maintain long-term residency in this home, and they were receptive to learning about efficiencies that could be installed during the building process. Instead of retrofitting the home at a later time, which might result in less aesthetically pleasing and more expensive options, we added simple features during the building process.

For example, in one of the bathrooms, we specified a Kohler Belay rail, which is a hidden handrail that looks like tile and ensures that you have a place to grab when you sense you are slipping in the shower.

Universal design can be timeless, allowing different generations to have a unique interpretation of the same design element. For example, the children began to describe the wheelchair access ramp at the back door as a skateboard ramp.

"Multi-Generational design is having the foresight to respect the various stages of your loved ones' lives . . ."

ROBIN WILSON

ELEVATOR

Due to the Kennedy family's long-term friendship with the late actor Christopher Reeve, they reflected upon the challenges he faced when their former home was accessible only by stairs, and he was in his wheelchair. It became very important to them that the home be accessible by more than stairs. The client wanted to install an elevator, which prompted many jokes and comments.

But after watching them pack for a family trip, it made complete sense to locate the elevator in the center of the home. Given the proximity to the luggage room, multiple bags can be packed and installed into a car by the housekeeping team.

Says Kamran Shushtarian, "As a mechanical engineer, our firm provided a residential elevator that would serve this family over many years. The hydraulic fluid is a derivative of vegetable oil, and the power usage is minimal. In addition, we have to remember that there is only one earth, and we need to preserve its resources and beauty for future generations."

This elevator will provide future access for the elderly or someone who is disabled. With this added accessibility to each floor, the home will remain useful indefinitely.

CURBLESS SHOWER

The most unique feature in the home is the ADA-compliant bath spa and powder room, which includes a curbless shower stall that allows a wheelchair to roll easily into the space. With a hand wand and a rain-shower head, the space provides comfortable access for anyone. Our goal was to manage aesthetic quality while ensuring both safety and accessibility.

We also installed a seat in many of the showers for ease of access and use and to ensure that there is a place to sit if a long shower is required. And both the steam and the sauna features of the spa will be helpful in the management of asthma and allergies as well as achy or arthritic joints at a later stage of life.

LIGHT SWITCH PLACEMENT

Our client came up with the brilliant idea of placing the light switches in every room at the same level as the doorknobs. This simple suggestion makes the home more accessible for all visitors and creates an intuitive reach location for the switches. This feature is an homage to the past, as this is the way it was done in most homes years ago.

ACCESSIBILITY

In addition, the closets and laundry rooms have baskets and hampers at easily accessible levels, plus at least one clothes rod at the proper height to accommodate someone who is wheelchair bound.

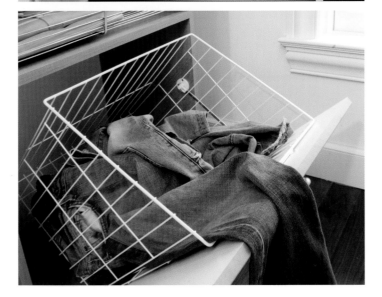

FLOORING

Dust accumulates on floors more than on any other surface. Keeping an allergy-free home means keeping your floors free of dust, which requires frequent cleaning—but it also means considering all your flooring options, and, if possible, using rugs instead of wall-to-wall carpets.

We selected eco-healthy flooring such as engineered hardwood, custom hardwood and tile. These smooth floor coverings are easier to keep dust-free, which prevents dust mites from multiplying and ensures that allergens are kept to an absolute minimum.

Certain flooring products, such as wall-to-wall carpet and vinyl flooring emit VOCs if they contain certain adhesives, backings, or sealants. It is important to know what type of flooring is in your home to prevent chemical off-gassing that can affect your indoor air quality.

HARDWOOD

Nothing beats hardwood. It's durable, rich and beautiful, and maintains its value for a lifetime. Hardwood flooring is harvested from the timber of such trees as oak, pine, maple, spruce and pecan. Because hardwood never goes out of style and offers a natural diversity of pattern and color unlike any other floor material—coupled with its health-related benefits—the Kennedy family's decision to use such flooring was an easy one to make.

When the house was demolished, they were able to salvage old flooring, and although the planks had to be recut into parquets, the entry hallway is a mix of reclaimed flooring in a very unique pattern, which pays homage to the former home and links the past to the present in the new home.

The exquisite custom hardwood flooring in the living room, dining room and study was designed by John Yarema flooring. It was reclaimed from original timber recycled from old barns and churches. The intricate detail in this floor is beautiful because of the design and the challenging pattern. Not only does this wood have a beautiful vintage look and feel, it also comes from first-generation trees, which are the strongest.

Any other wood flooring in the home was Forest Stewardship Council (FSC)-certified to ensure that it came from sustainably managed forests. This means that a tree was planted whenever another tree was felled to manufacture flooring.

BAMBOO

The kitchen floor is caramelized bamboo with a matte finish. Bamboo is a grass and is thus sustainable—and it comes in hundreds of species. As you will read in the Green Pages, this non-toxic and pesticide-free grass product is used in flooring more frequently. A matte finish was used, and this darkened color allows the bamboo to blend more easily into the custom hardwood flooring.

COBBLEWOOD

The service hall, mudroom and main laundry room off the kitchen was designed by Birger Juell, Ltd. The floor uses the butt ends of rough timber—called cobblewood—that is traditionally discarded or burned by sawmills. This highly durable floor is often seen in ski lodges. It can stand up to the wear and tear of ski boots, so you know it can handle lots of family members and guests.

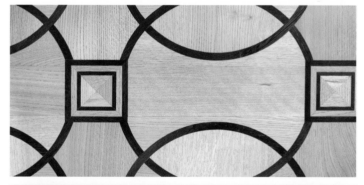

CUSTOM

As aforementioned, the custom flooring in the living room, dining room and RFK study came from the work of John Yarema, based in Detroit, who is often the winner of "best floor" awards.

ENGINEERED

Mohawk makes an engineered laminate floor that works well with radiant heat systems. Sometimes standard hardwood will expand and contract dependent upon heat and moisture content, and the engineered flooring will remain in perfect condition for many years.

CARPETS

Many of the carpets are made by Karastan and contain recycled nylon fibers from old carpets that were once destined for landfills. Says Jenny Cross of Mohawk Industries (which manufactures engineered flooring, Dal-Tile and Karastan carpets), "I believe that green or eco-friendly practices are important because they are choices which give back and ultimately live on after us. Conservation and eco-conscious living will allow a more sustainable planet for generations to come. Our greatest challenge on this project was balancing style with performance needs. This project was unique and demanding, so we had to choose the perfect product to live up to that challenge."

With six children, and regular entertaining, the family was very concerned about the durability of the carpets, and since the Karastan product had been specified in their home prior to this project, they knew that it was a quality product. Upon learning about the company's renewed commitment to the environment, the family was thrilled to accept the donation of the carpeting for various rooms in the home.

PAGE 142: Stair treads of quarter-sawn oak.

PAGE 143: (clockwise from top left): Reclaimed wood prior to treatment; workshop cleaning/curing; Yarema team installing floor; John Yarema reviewing before stain application.

HARDWOOD

OPTION | 1

Nothing beats hardwood. It is durable, rich and beautiful, and maintains its value for a lifetime. Hardwood boasts a natural diversity of pattern and color unlike any other floor material. Look for wood with an FSC certification to ensure sustainable forestry practices. Flooring is harvested from timber of trees such as oak, pecan, maple, spruce and pine. It is renewable, but beware of harmful logging practices. A budget-conscious product to consider is an engineered wood product made by Mohawk, a company that maintains sustainable practices during its manufacturing process. An engineered flooring product also works well with radiant heat.

BAMBOO

OPTION | 2

Bamboo is an eco-healthy alternative to hardwood flooring, and it looks quite similar. However, bamboo is actually a grass that grows up to a meter a day for some species. The grass is harvested and then kiln dried. It also stands up to humidity, and the mature species have the durability of hardwood. We used Dragonfly caramelized bamboo in the kitchen and family room because of its hypoallergenic properties and the wide variety of wide-plank options using the Moso species, which is the hardest variety of bamboo. Install flooring using non-formaldehyde glues and ensure that an anti-scratch UV coating is applied.

CORK

OPTION | 3

Cork is a natural and resilient flooring option that is also great for sound minimization. Cork floors are made from the bark of cork oak trees, which are sustainably grown on plantations. Cork is a renewable resource—the bark returns after it is harvested and can be re-harvested after seven to ten years. Cork is recyclable, biodegradable and does not release toxic gas. Because it comes in tiles, it can actually be taken with you if you move. It is not recommended for use in basements where it may be susceptible to mold.

IMAGE COURTESY OF GLOBUS CORK

LINOLEUM

OPTION | 4

Linoleum is back as an eco-healthy flooring option, although it has been rebranded as Marmoleum. It is durable, biodegradable and comfortable, yet quiet when one walks across floor. This is not your grandmother's linoleum—there are fifty-plus newly created patterns and colors. It is made from natural materials such as felt, burlap or canvas coated with linseed oil and comes in either sheets, strips or tiles. It is hypo-allergenic and anti-static, meaning it repels dust and dirt, and if you have chemical sensitivities, be aware of a natural off-gassing scent that will go away over time.

IMAGE COURTESY OF FORBO

CONCRETE

OPTION | 5

Concrete slab foundations are being finished as floors and the designs go well beyond the standard gray. Made from a mixture of cement, water, sand/gravel and fly ash in some cases, it is an eco-material. It is impossible to damage. We kept the original poured foundation of the home in an area off the pool and outdoor loggia, where wet feet and dripping swimsuits will make a regular path. With radiant flooring and the ability of concrete to maintain a constant temperature, we believe this will lower utility bills. It is also a great choice for those suffering from allergies or asthma and requires minimal cleaning.

STONE

OPTION | 6

Stone is a natural material that is virtually free of VOCs. We used stone in the entry vestibule as an attractive surface that is easily swept or mopped. Says Ilene Lush of Chelsea Arts Tile & Stone, "There are so many stone varieties with various options in size, color, texture. When selected from a well-managed quarry, stone is a great alternative to ceramic for the home or office space." When going for LEED certification, it is better to reuse stone versus using stone from a first-generation quarry. The strength and simplicity of stone has made it a long-time favorite of designers and architects.

TILE

OPTION 7

Tile is one of the oldest flooring materials, dating to over 6,000 years ago. The Dal-Tile showroom experts note: "Eco-projects typically use glass, porcelain or ceramic tile." Ceramic tile is made from clay and then fired in a kiln, with an optional glaze application. Porcelain tile is kiln fired at a higher temperature and comes in multiple patterns, textures and sizes. Glass tile is made from new (clear or frosted) or recycled opaque artisan glass, which can be used on walls or floors. Setting most tile in cement is the best option for indoor air quality and more durable than adhesives.

RUGS & CARPETS

OPTION 8

Rugs and carpets are key elements in this home, given the amount of hardwood and concrete. These textiles will ensure that spaces are cozy, comfortable and sound absorbent. We selected natural fibers that were affixed to natural fiber backings with low-VOC glues. The healthiest carpets are those made from untreated 100 percent wood, cotton, sisal, hemp or sea grass. All carpets that are healthy options will not off-gas with irritating or harmful fumes after installation. Says the Karastan team, "We actually recycle the nylon fibers from old carpets to ensure sustainable practices while making our new carpets."

ENERGY EFFICIENCY

CHAPTER | 13

The most powerful argument for building an eco-friendly home comes from lowered energy usage. With so much technological advancement in lighting and geothermal, solar and hybrid forms of power, this living laboratory will become an opportunity to calculate energy savings. As consumer demand increases, it is our hope that pricing will be lowered to ensure more affordable options in the market, thus decreasing the payback timeframe.

Ultimately, the Kennedys chose to use radiant heat, geothermal power, and passive solar power; high-tech lighting, newspaper and soybean sealant insulation; and a hybrid hot water heater in their home.

Given the family's commitment to lowering their dependence on fossil fuels, this chapter will be an exciting learning tool for those who want to minimize their home's environmental impact.

Says Brooks Washburn, "An interesting potential feature of this home is the ability to connect to and respond to the larger environment's energy needs and uses: if excess electricity is generated by the home, or if electricity (through a future smart-grid software) is needed elsewhere, the power can be placed into the grid. And if the home is using electricity from the grid and there are supply limitations, the home can respond to the commands of the smart-grid and diminish or time the use of electricity from the grid into the home. A strong feature of the design is the transfer of existing energy into and around the house—and exhaust air from the building is on a timed system to maintain indoor air quality for health, but the air is vented through a heat exchanger to capture the heat energy from the existing air and preheat the incoming fresh air."

LIGHTING

The Kennedy project team recognized that this home has multiple lighting needs—from task to spot lighting, ambient to accent lighting, and energy-efficient to low-UV lighting. Given that incandescent bulbs are on the verge of extinction, it became clear that "acronym oriented" bulbs (LED, CFL, etc.) would become de rigueur during the lighting design process. It has become common knowledge that the incandescent bulb is being phased out in Europe. We understand that this will soon be the case in the United States due to the inefficiency of these bulbs.

Some experts have described incandescent bulbs as space heaters that give light as a by-product, which wastes much of the power through heat emissions. Replacing one 75-watt incandescent bulb with an 18-watt compact fluorescent (CFL) will, over the lifespan of the new bulb, save one ton of carbon dioxide and 8 kilograms of sulphur dioxide from being emitted into the atmosphere. In addition, CFLs save tremendously on electricity costs, and the bulbs last ten times longer than do incandescent bulbs. (Source: Rocky Mountain Power Institute)

Our clients wanted energy-efficient lighting, but they also wanted to ensure that it was neither too blue nor white, given that some energy-efficient lighting is not up to par with the desired light quality. The complaints leveled against light-emitting diodes (LEDs) or CFLs result from bulbs that do not have a sufficient Kelvin temperature, quality of light, or candle lumens. Our eyes have been trained to see the yellows and pinks of incandescent bulbs, and some energy-efficient bulbs show results in an aquarium-like hue, which is not pleasant in a residential environment.

With so much technological advancement in lighting, we realized that the Kennedy home could become a showplace for the latest innovations. The builder and design team suggested a combination of options: LEDs, low voltage, passive, and fiber-optic lights.

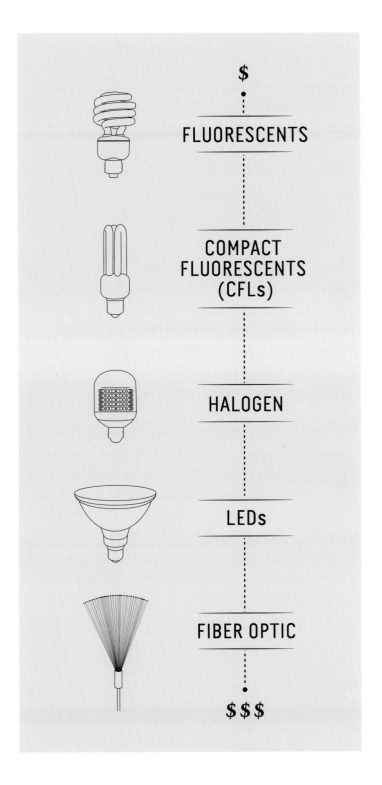

$

FLUORESCENTS

COMPACT
FLUORESCENTS
(CFLs)

HALOGEN

LEDs

FIBER OPTIC

$ $ $

The Kennedy home has a gallery wall of amazing art and signed works that could fade in the presence of UV light emissions, so we decided to use fiber-optic lighting in the upper hallway, which is one of the most efficient technologies. A single light source in a device the size of a shoebox allows light to refract approximately sixteen feet to small apertures that spotlight without any heat radiation.

Says Sandra Liotus, "Liotus Lighting Design was invited to donate museum quality, energy-efficient fiber-optic lighting for the second level of the home, which will highlight a historical document collection of autographs from presidents and dictators. According to the clients, these historical documents have a tendency to irretrievably fade if subjected to conventional lighting."

The Liotus Lighting team installed an SL-150 glass fiber-optic system that filters both the infrared and ultraviolet areas of the spectrum, leaving only the visible portion. The documents will be able to be lit into posterity without the danger of destruction. It is clear that the benefit of the system is that the relative humidity is not altered by lighting, thus removing the possibility of the documents becoming dried out or brittle. Two light sources hidden in closets project their light through custom-made fused common end glass harnesses. Each light source generates a total of 12,500 lumens in the visible spectrum and uses a very high-efficiency, color stabilized and balanced metal halide 150-watt lamp with a life of 8000 hours.

The power of the fiber-optic system is that only two lamps have to be changed for the entire 40-foot corridor. Each of the fittings is also hand-crafted from solid metal and is capable of directional adjustment of 45 degrees in any vertical direction—controlling the focus and spreading the light between a tight spot and full wash of light.

> "The world cannot continue to allow its resources to be squandered at the current rate, or allow future generations to inherit a polluted, inefficient world."
>
> SANDRA LIOTUS

At some point, the family will be able to link the lighting into a Crestron smart-house system. According to Sandra Liotus, "The system has been very successfully designed into the residences of many of the world's most renowned art collectors due to its conservation properties allowing for the most valuable art to be correctly and evenly illuminated—even in the most inaccessible locations. As well, this SL-150 system saves considerable amounts of energy, future maintenance and material waste. Most importantly, the entire system is fully sustainable and all components are capable of being 100 percent recycled. And given the fact that no heat is emitted from the fiber-optic output fittings, there is no load on the cooling system."

Technically, the fiber-optic system uses only 336 watts of electricity, and the light output is equivalent to 900 watts of tungsten halogen lighting. As there are only two light sources, each with a running life of 8000 hours, it is calculated that 128 low-voltage lamps are saved during this period in addition to the 564 watts of electricity saved in comparison to a standard low-voltage lamp system.

Using fiber-optic lighting in the Kennedy construction project was the easiest way to implement lighting efficiency, and it was good to know that they are able to retrofit existing homes when improper or inefficient lighting has been used.

Center hallway on second level with Solatubes and fiber optic light apertures.

LIGHT-EMITTING DIODES (LEDS)

The LED bulb is the newest and most technologically advanced product. It includes bulbs that fit into a standard housing, recessed lights, ribbon strips, task lighting, nightlights, and flashlights. The newest LED product is called an organic LED, which is a thin sheet of light that is being tested for television sets and watch faces. This technology is seen in residences too because it is a low-temperature bulb and therefore especially safe to use for undermounted kitchen lights and within millwork.

LOW VOLTAGE

The typical reference to low-voltage lighting considers both fluorescent and halogen bulbs.

- The fluorescent is the most efficient, and there are two types: standard (workspace) and compact (home). The biggest issue with these bulbs is that they are improperly disposed of because most people don't know that the bulbs contain mercury in trace amounts. When they are not disposed of properly, mercury can leach into a landfill, thus poisoning waterways.

- The halogen bulb is used most often in outdoor applications where temperature can be an issue, or in specific task or spot lighting applications such as a backsplash or art wall in a home.

Energy consumption on a global basis is one of the most compelling current political and environmental issues. The following list describes today's energy sources:

CORE BASELOAD POWER

FOSSIL FUELS (coal, natural gas, diesel) the goal is to reduce reliance on these natural, non-renewable resources

HYDRO-POWER ("dam storage") can have substantial storage capacity, but can wreak havoc on natural flow of waterways and biodiversity

NUCLEAR is a controversial power option due to safety issues and hazardous waste generation

GEOTHERMAL means "hot earth" and is a renewable resource from the heat generated from the core of the earth

INTERMITTENT POWER

SOLAR is processed through photovoltaic panels with constant power generated during day and excess power storage in batteries for nighttime usage

WIND is sometimes unreliable, and site specific, working best in cold air climates

HYDROPOWER ("run of river") can have limited or no storage capacity and is sometimes dependent upon rain or snowmelts, but does not have as much impact on local ecological systems

BIOMASS is based on the combustion of crops or crop residue; renewable power source dependent upon waste collection

PASSIVE

We have installed Solatubes in the ceiling of the entire second level of the of the house, where the private quarters are located. This passive lighting system works through a mushroom-shaped prism on the rooftop that allows light to enter an interior tube of mirrors and reflectors, culminating in non-UV light entering an aperture in the home. These Solatubes are located in the center hall and ensure that lights do not have to be turned on during the day.

In addition, each closet is outfitted with a Solatube, which means that each morning, lights do not have to be turned on while the family members get dressed. However, on an extremely cloudy day or at night, the aperture contains an LED or CFL bulb that can be turned on, without requiring a second opening in the ceiling. At night, the system can be dimmed if you don't want light seepage under the closet door in the morning.

SOLAR POWER

Solar power lowers energy costs to both utilities and consumers with efficient production of clean energy. And given the many state certification programs in existence today, homeowners benefit because they often receive tax credits for use of solar power.

One way to capture this energy is through the use of photovoltaics (PVs). *Photovoltaic* is a combined form of the Greek word for light and the name Alessandro Volta, a late-eighteenth-century Italian physicist. Says architect Brooks Washburn, "The solar hot water panels capture heat and light from the sun on the roof and transfer it to the system powering the domestic hot water. The south-facing windows capture solar heat in the winter and with the exception of the hybrid hot water system used as a backup, there is no direct use of fossil fuel in the building for space or domestic water heating. Net energy use has been reduced passively through south-facing windows and sun-control devices."

In simple terms, as sunlight strikes the surface of a PV cell, some of the light's photons are absorbed. The result is that electrons are released from the cell, further resulting in a generation of voltage, or flow of electricity. PV technologies use flat plates, the components of which focus the sunlight onto smaller and more efficient cells. This type of power generates no air pollution or hazardous waste, and given the global uncertainty regarding fossil fuels, this renewable energy source is a winner for consumers who want to save money. Each kilowatt hour of PV-produced electricity offset up to 830

pounds of nitrogen oxide, 1,500 pounds of sulfur dioxide, and 217,000 pounds of carbon dioxide. (Source: National Renewable Energy Lab)

PVs are also referred to as solar cells, which contain semiconductor materials that can be connected to form an array. Contrary to popular thought, these PV panels generate power in all types of weather, with 80 percent of energy generation on a partly cloudy day and even 25 percent on extremely overcast days.

It is indicated that within a decade, PV power may be competitive in price with traditional electricity sources. Consumers are getting more attracted to this as an option because the solar cells are getting smaller: large roof panels used to be the only size available, but PVs are now found in wristwatches, calculators, and backpack-size products. For example, in 2001 Home Depot began selling solar cells in San Diego, and due to customer demand, by 2002 they had expanded sales to more than sixty stores nationwide.

Although a small amount of energy is lost when converting DC electricity to AC, the converter allows the solar-cell generation to integrate in a way similar to utility grid power for efficient operation of appliances, lights and computers.

Solar shingles are the newest way to ensure an alternative power source while maintaining an aesthetically pleasing home.

GEOTHERMAL

The most exciting system used within this home creates both power and warmth without environmental pollution—and at a considerable cost savings over time. *Geothermal* is derived from the Greek words *geo* (earth) and *thermos* (heat) and means power extracted from the heat stored in the earth. The premise underlying this system is to maintain a steady interior temperature of 58 degrees Fahrenheit—the earth's core temperature—all year-round. Imagine wanting to heat your home to 65 degrees when it is 30 degrees outside. If you use conventional heating methods, you would have to raise the temperature in your home 38 degrees, while the geothermal heat pump system would need to raise it only 7 degrees.

When we see a geyser or hot spring, we are able to easily comprehend the surface effects of geothermal heat. An even more dramatic visual demonstration of geothermal heat is a volcano erupting and spewing molten lava. In Roman times, geothermal water was used to heat buildings, and in North America, Native Americans used hot spring water for medicinal purposes and cooking.

The geothermal power used in a home comes from the geothermal wells that are drilled into the earth's core to actuate the water trapped in underground cracks and porous rock—called a geothermal reservoir.

In the United States, engineers and geologists locate geothermal reservoirs to which they can connect heat pumps, often called "heat exchangers." These exchangers transfer the heat to water pipes, which circulate the warm water in the building's heating system. The heated water then travels (we used radiant heat for the flooring) to a coolant area (the family has a free heated swimming pool!) before being injected back into the well to be heated once again and used repeatedly.

The U.S. Environmental Protection Agency has rated geothermal heat pumps (GHPs) as one of the most efficient methods of heating and cooling. The weather does not change the basic technologic premise of this system:

- Heating: Earth heat is transferred to the continuously circulating water, thus heating the building.

- Cooling: Building heat is transferred to the continuously circulating water, thus cooling it and discharging heat back into earth.

Geothermal power is sustainable, low-cost and eco-friendly and could be used more universally in place of fossil fuels. In the future, it is expected that there will be more development of geothermal plants around the world. As of 2004 more than seventy countries used geothermal heating, and it is predicted globally that 40% will use heat pumps in residential construction by 2020.

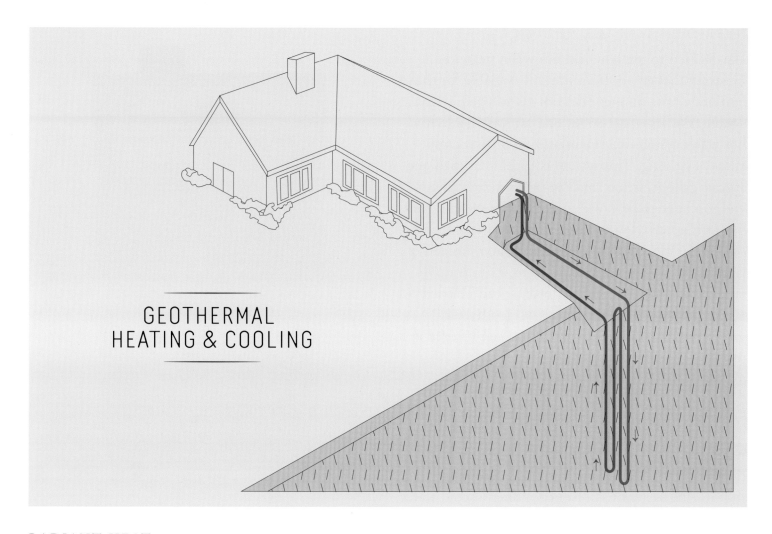

GEOTHERMAL
HEATING & COOLING

RADIANT HEAT

A by-product of the geothermal system is the low-cost heat that warms the flooring in the home, which ensures comfort in winter and increases the heating capacity, since heat rises and flooring can often remain cold. In this home, each room has radiant heat beneath the flooring surface, which should increase comfort for occupants.

HYBRID HOT WATER HEATER

We decided to use a hybrid hot water heater to illustrate that eco-options are still available for those families whose budget does not allow a geothermal system. For less than $600, one can install a hybrid hot water system that maintains an 86% thermal efficiency rating. This system is LEED-certified and at four gallons, is too small to be considered a tank and too large to be called tankless. The system works by storing heated water, and when someone turns on a water tap, there is instant hot water, instead of running water for a few minutes to warm it up—and wasting precious gallons over a year. This hybrid is a support/backup system for the geothermal system in the Kennedy home, but it can be used as a primary system for any home.

This system constantly supplies hot water for everyone, and during peak shower times, it will not lose water pressure or have temperature fluctuations, which are problems sometimes found in tank and tankless units. The system also has a computer monitoring system to prevent scalding or cold water shock which is common with older water heaters on the market.

Says Paul Home of Grand Hall USA, "I believe that eco-friendly practices are important because they usher in a new thought leadership, a smarter living process, and as a society, we should continually be working to incorporate smarter appliances that use less energy. If we are able to have the same comforts while using less, we will have truly succeeded." And at an affordable price point, this can be an alternative to a geothermal application.

Cellulose (news-paper) insulation provides excellent coverage for walls; enlarged image shows writing on a piece of newspaper.

INSULATION

The bottom line for any home that will be evaluated for an energy efficiency rating (EER) is the level of insulation—a basic, yet often overlooked element in the design process. Insulation is a core requirement for the eco-friendly home to ensure that heating and cooling occur without loss to the exterior. Simply put, it makes little sense to turn up your thermostat if you have a poorly insulated home, which over-burdens the power plant and costs you money. Our clients were deeply committed to researching and understanding all of the insulation options available.

The in-wall insulation is recycled from shredded newspapers by Green Star, and the exterior blanket and high-tech sheeting insulation provided by Dow.

Before the sheetrock was applied to cover the newspapers, you could actually read a bit of the news, although in short snippets. Says Bobby, "One idle day while browsing my walls, I was dismayed to discover a byline of right wing columnist Cal Thomas and the masthead of the *Washington Times* just above my master bedroom window. I console myself that my home has inadvertently performed a public service by permanently interring a coleslaw library of conservative blather behind impenetrable sheetrock."

INCANDESCENT BULBS

OPTION | 1

The incandescent bulb is being phased out of usage in Europe currently and will be phased out globally, although it will always be recognized as the original source of electric lighting. The bulbs work by heating a solid filament wire until it glows—much like a space heater—and this is an inefficient use of electricity. However, this technology has been used for over 100 years and although manufactured inexpensively, the lights can increase the heat load in a building, which adds to cooling costs.

IMAGE COURTESY OF WESTINGHOUSE LIGHTING CO.

CFL BULBS

OPTION | 2

Compact fluorescent (CFL) bulbs have been a strong middle option for consumers, and these low-voltage bulbs with the funny shape are quite affordable. However, the biggest downside to the use of the bulbs is that they contain mercury in minute concentrations. And when the bulbs are disposed of in a landfill, the mercury can enter a landfill and be washed into waterways during a rain, thus causing toxic contaminants to enter water streams and marine life. These bulbs use a little more energy when first turned on, but use around 75% less electricity than a standard incandescent bulb.

IMAGE COURTESY OF WESTINGHOUSE LIGHTING CO.

LED LIGHTING

OPTION | 3

The strongest breakout trend for residential consumers is the use of light-emitting diodes (LED) lights that outlast regular bulbs by 30x and can light a stairway or external area all night for less power than a single incandescent bulb uses in two hours. LEDs also produce more light per watt than standard incandescent bulbs. The biggest barrier to their widespread adoption had been the spectrum of light was too blue or white, thus leading to an aquarium feel. However, with modern innovations, the cost is affordable to more consumers with recessed and light bulb options introduced in 2009.

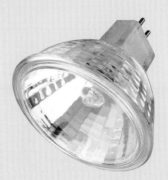

LOW-VOLTAGE HALOGEN

OPTION | 4

Halogen lights are more compact than incandescent bulbs and produce more lumens per bulb, although with some heat output. Typically, the bulbs allow a wide spectrum or a pinpoint spotlight. Because the bulbs can work at a very low energy use, a simple way to understand is that a 50-watt low-voltage halogen bulb can produce the same lumens for a 125-watt bulb. It is important to consider bulbs that are frosted or tinted, as clear bulbs are typically used in retail stores and produce a very harsh light.

FIBER OPTICS

OPTION | 5

More consumers are using fiber-optic lights in their homes, as they use up to 8x less energy than a standard incandescent bulb. Additionally, they do not generate heat, which can lower cooling bills. As costs come down, we are seeing the use of the bulbs in pools, walkways and as task lighting. Plus, for those who have precious artwork or autographs, the bulbs do not emit UV rays, which ensures no fading of text or color spectrum. Fiber optic lights can emit 90 lumens per watt (without heat emission), while a standard incandescent will produce 15 lumens per watt.

SOLATUBE

OPTION | 6

It is not a skylight, but a passive lighting device that allows light to enter into places where natural light had not been an option. Using a system of mirrors and reflectors, the light enters a dome- shaped prism on the roof of a building and is propelled into an interior space, without any heat or UV rays. For a center hall home, this is a way to prevent use of electricity during the day, plus in a location such as a closet, it eliminates the peak demand during morning rush hour. And this product is eligible for federal tax credits upon installation!

IMAGE COURTESY OF SOLATUBE

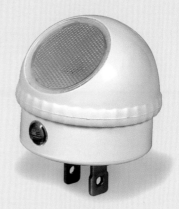

NIGHT LIGHTS

OPTION 7

The most eco-friendly night lights are LED lights. They use less than one watt of power and last up to 30,000 hours. Some models are light-sensitive so that they automatically turn off when the ambient light reaches a certain level. And the bulbs will not shatter if dropped. The easiest way to describe the quality of this light is to think of them as the type of light technology used to power laptop screens. Low cost to operate, no added heat for your cooling bill, and low additional waste to a landfill because they last for years!

IMAGE COURTESY OF MAXXIMA LED

WIND-UP LIGHTS

OPTION 8

For the most ardent environmentalist, the eco-friendly wind-up LED or xenon flashlight allows an emergency light anytime, and no fear that a battery will be dead. A quick crank of the handle allows approximately eight minutes of light. But some of the smaller versions for a handbag have only one or two LEDs inside and can work for hours. As more people commit to using less power, this is a great option as opposed to plugging in a rechargeable flashlight every day (and using phantom power!). A better option in case there is a power outage is the wind-up flashlight.

IMAGE COURTESY OF KIKKERLAND DESIGN

SUSTAINABILITY

CHAPTER | 14

The definition of sustainability within the context of an eco-healthy home is: *living within the capacity of the ecosystem with the ability to endure or maintain over time.* Sustainable practices for the home are quite simple and based upon the adoption of the three R's: recycling, reusing objects (so they remain out of the landfill), and renewable energy.

The Industrial Revolution, from the 19th to the 20th century, resulted in the expanded use of fossil fuels for machinery, technology and urban centers. After World War II, the interstate highway system influenced urban planning: populations concentrated in high-rises in the metropolitan areas that evolved from town centers and there was growth in the suburbs connected by the new expressways. During this time, there was a rise in the technology for and usage of synthetics, chemicals, plastics and nuclear energy.

Into that industrial development came a nascent environmental movement heralded by the publication in 1962 of the pivotal book *Silent Spring* by Rachel Carson. There was finally a growing awareness of the human impact on the environment. During the late 1970s to the mid-1980s, sparked by the 1979 energy crisis, we saw President Jimmy Carter place solar panels on the White House roof (only to see them removed by the next administration). We also saw more research into hydroelectricity, wind power and geothermal resources. Although we did not have the opportunity to use wind power on the Kennedys' home, it must be mentioned that more people are adding this element to their homes. Also, many municipalities are utilizing wind as an alternative to fossil fuels.

Says architect Brooks Washburn, "There was a reduction in the embodied energy in the construction itself: many materials were produced locally or within LEED guidelines, such as brick and flooring; many materials are reused, such as the slate roof and doors; and many materials are recycled, such as much of the old foundation, which was crushed and used as gravel. Materials were selected to reduce their life-cycle cost and diminish future replacement cost burdens, through durable, long-lasting and low-maintenance materials (brick, wood flooring, slate roof).

RECYCLING

Furniture is the most visible and newest focus of the sustainability movement. It is important to look for items that have the Forest Stewardship Council (FSC) label, which means that a tree is planted each time one is taken down. Paulette Cole of ABC Carpet & Home, says, "ABC Home has pioneered the cause of social responsibility by endorsing sustainability in products and taking stands on global environment and health issues."

> "My role was to recommend flooring that met the Kennedys' need for green, style and performance."
>
> JENNY CROSS
> *Director of Sustainability,*
> *Mohawk Industries*

With such a strong environmental commitment, the Kennedys made sure their home is also a laboratory for easy-to-emulate lifestyle options. A recycling center was designed into the kitchen as a visible example of how to incorporate this practice into your standard routine in a stylish design. There were two types of recycled hardwood flooring installed in the home: engineered and custom. The wide-plank engineered floor is in all of the bedrooms and works well with radiant floors. Says Jenny Cross, "The Kennedys' insightful choice to use radiant heating on the upper floor limited the types of flooring that could be installed. The collaboration between Mohawk, Robin and Mary to find the perfect style choice which also fit the technical needs was truly rewarding. At the end of the day we chose a beautiful floor that was economical and met all of Mary's needs and budget."

The custom flooring was installed using reclaimed barn wood and the last bits of flooring from the original home that were not infested with black mold. These pieces were cleaned and cut into parquets so that a bit of the former home is part of the new home.

Says architect Brooks Washburn, "I believe that eco-friendly practices are important because there must be limits. Americans seem to be using too much, casually and unselfconsciously . . . and the developing world probably cannot imitate our historical pattern. Within the limits of the environment to supply the desired resources or to accept the result of these resources (pollution, carbon gases), there seems to be evidence and experience that happiness is not directly affected by increased or decreased consumption. It must be seen that the 'new cool' is to live sustainably . . . and the 'what if we don't' gamble may be too great a risk given potential harm from future generations. My greatest challenge was balancing the performance aspects of the technical system with the aesthetic demands of the classic home style . . ."

REUSING

As you view the slate roof tiles and first level doors, you will know that this fifty-plus-year-old building material was saved and reused on the home. These tiles were donated by Allan Shope, who is the curator of a parcel of land that was once occupied by Wassaic mental institutions, which were decommissioned in the 1980s. Instead of throwing everything into the landfill, he saved key elements which are being reused in this home.

> "Gains on projects such as this have their absolute measurable value as well as their symbolic value."
>
> BROOKS WASHBURN
> *Lead Architect*

In addition, the Kennedy property is rich in natural resources, from its wetlands to a waterfront lake to its forest and indigenous rock. Rather than import rock from another location, the stonemasons handled this project the old-fashioned way by blasting a big rock on the property. The smaller pieces were chiseled, as needed, for a perfect fit around the exterior of the home.

RENEWABLE ENERGY

At the start of this project, the Kennedy family indicated that they wanted to use solar power and geothermal power in the home. As you have read in this chapter, the excitement around the technological innovations made this a huge contribution to the project.

Residential heating and cooling make up 20% of the annual energy usage of the United States. Homes are giants in consumption with appliances and electronics, but by using efficient light bulbs, solar power and geothermal power, this home will contribute positively to the living environment.

On the southern face of the roof, the solar shingle array blends in elegantly with the multi-colored stone slate tiles from the former mental institutions. Says Bobby, "These slick new photovoltaic shingles power our electric system night and day with energy stored in a cutting-edge, non-toxic battery manufactured by Premium Power. And with our Enmax solar thermal system, water is heated at zero cost for our entire family and frequent guests. Our home is a power plant that will allow us to participate in the 'new energy' economy while minting enormous cost savings for our family."

Says the chief electrician, Fred Carboni of Franklin Electric, "I believe that green or eco-friendly practices are important because they demonstrate respect and appreciation of the limited resources available to us on the planet Earth. The families that choose to go green are required to make a deliberate lifestyle change that is uncommon in our fast-paced, throw-away society. My greatest challenge was working to stay on pace with the tight timeline and having the opportunity to see the awesome features within the walls makes me hope that this will become the norm for building houses of the future."

Solar shingles from rooftop.

DESIGN EPILOGUE

All hardwood furniture and cabinetry selected for the home used formaldehyde-free adhesives. We identified companies who support sustainable forestry practices (planting a new tree when using a tree during the manufacturing process), and those who use sustainable materials and manufacturing processes to preserve the environment.

And finally, one of our favorite excursions was to vintage shops and antique barns to identify items that are unique and one of a kind, such as vintage typewriters, accessory tables and vintage toys.

We truly appreciate the participation of all the generous sponsors who believed in this project.

The Kennedy Green House will remain a pivotal landmark where "classic design meets eco-innovation" and we appreciate this opportunity to share their beautiful home with you . . .

ROBIN WILSON

RESOURCE GUIDE

ASSOCIATIONS

The American Institute of Architects
Washington, DC
+ (800) 242-3837
www.aia.org

American Society of Interior Designers
Washington, DC
+ (202) 546-3480
www.asid.org

Asthma & Allergy Foundation of America
Washington, DC
+ (800) 727-8462
www.aafa.org

Natural Resources Defense Council
New York, NY
+ (212) 727-2700
www.nrdc.org

U.S. Environmental Protection Agency
Washington, DC
www.epa.gov

U.S. Green Building Council
Washington, DC
www.usgbc.org

TRADE SHOWS

Architectural Digest Home Show
New York, NY 10001
+ (800) 677-6278
www.archdigesthomeshow.com

Go Green Expo
New York, NY
+ (212) 655-4505
www.gogreenexpo.com

Greenbuild
Washington, DC
+ (800) 795-1747
www.greenbuildexpo.org

Kitchen Bath International Show (KBIS)
+ (800) 933-8735
www.kbis.com

APPLIANCES

Electrolux
local dealers nationwide
www.electrolux.com

ARCHITECTS

Patrick M. Croke, Architect
Bedford, NY
+ (914) 234-6093
www.pmcarchitect.com

William McDonough
Charlottesville, VA
+ (434) 979-1111
www.mcdonough.com

Allan Shope Architect
Wassaic, NY
+ (845) 877-6335
www.shopearchitect.com

Brooks Washburn
Potsdam, NY
+ (315) 268-1338
www.brookswashburnarchitect.com

BUILDING TEAM

Blansfield Builders
Roxbury, CT
+ (203) 797-9174
www.blansfieldbuilders.com

B&D Controlled Air Corp.
New Milford, CT
+ (860) 355-3705
www.bdair.com

Botticelli Plumbing
Danbury, CT
+ (203) 794-9297
www.botticelliplumbingandheating.com

Franklin Electric
Danbury, CT
+ (203) 746-5088

Nick Scattolini & Son Painting
Oxford, CT
+ (203) 264-1305

Stone Ridge Excavation
Bethel, CT
+ (203) 797-8182

Zini Masonry
New Fairfield, CT
+ (203) 746-2570

BUILDING SUPPLY

Chelsea Arts Tile + Stone
New York, NY
+ (646) 638-0444
www.chelseaartstileandstone.com

ECO Supply
Brooklyn, NY
+ (800) 883-7005
www.ecosupplycenter.com

Marvin Windows and Doors
local dealers nationwide
+ (888) 537-7828
www.marvin.com

The Millennium Collection
local dealers nationwide
+ (888) 454-8888
www.milleniumdoors.com

Ring's End Lumber
Darien, CT
+ (800) 390-1000
www.ringsend.com

The Stiles and Hart Brick Company
Bridgewater, MA
+ (800) 320-8700
www.stilesandhart.com

3form
showrooms nationwide
www.3-form.com

CABINETRY

Holiday Kitchens
local dealers nationwide
www.holidaykitchens.com

Enda Kelly Woodworking
Yonkers, NY
+ (914) 965-4059

CAR SHARING

Zipcar
locations nationwide
+ (866) 494-7227
www.zipcar.com

CLEANING SUPPLIES

Method
local stores nationwide
+ (866) 963-8463
www.methodhome.com

CLOSETS

EasyClosets
Pine Brook, NJ
+ (800) 910-0129
www.easyclosets.com

COUNTERTOPS

ECO by Cosentino
local showrooms nationwide
+ (866) 579-4326
www.ecobycosentino.com

PaperStone
local showrooms nationwide
+ (360) 538-9815
www.paperstoneproducts.com

ELEVATOR

Mobility Elevator & Lift Co.
+ (800) 441-4181
www.mobilityelevator.com

FIREPLACES

Amendola Stone & Fabrication (hearthstones)
White Plains, NY
+ (914) 997-7968
www.amendolamarble.net

Majestic Fireplaces
local dealers nationwide
www.majesticproducts.com

FLOORING

Birger Juell, Ltd.
Chicago, IL
+ (312) 464-9663
www.birgerjuell.com

Dragonfly Bamboo
local dealers nationwide
www.dragonflybamboo.com

Mohawk Flooring
local dealers nationwide
+ (800) 266-4295
www.mohawkflooring.com

Karastan
local dealers nationwide
+ (800) 234-1120
www.karastan.com

Yarema Creative Hardwood Flooring
Detroit, MI
+ (248) 798-8388
www.johnyarema.com

FLOWERS

Forever In Bloom
Mt. Kisco, NY
+ (914) 241-1963
www.foreverinbloomonline.com

FURNITURE

ABC Carpet & Home
New York
+ (212) 473-3000
www.abchome.com

Anderson Pews
Zeeland, MI
+ (616) 292-4125
www.church-furnishings.com

Bisley Office Cabinets & Lockers
local dealers worldwide
+ (718) 627-5905
www.bisley.com

BoConcept
Scarsdale, NY
+ (914) 472-2535
www.boconcept.com

Jeff Bridgman Antiques
Historic York County, Pennsylvania
+ (717) 502-1281
www.jeffbridgman.com

Mitchell Gold + Bob Williams
local showrooms nationwide
+ (212) 431-2575
www.mgandbw.com

Somnium
Venice, CA
+ (323) 655-6700
www.somniumbeds.com

The Nest Store
online retail store
+ (866) 885-6584
www.theneststore.com

VivaTerra
online retail store
+ (800) 233-6011
www.vivaterra.com

HOUSEWARES (TABLETOP)

ABC Carpet & Home
New York, NY
+ (212) 473-3000
www.abchome.com

ECOBAGS
Ossining, NY
+ (800) 720-2247
www.ecobags.com

Fishs Eddy
New York, NY
+ (212) 420-9020
www.fishseddy.com

Gracious Home
New York, NY
+ (212) 231-7800
www.gracioushome.com

Hangers.com
online retail store
+ (800) 573-1445
www.hangers.com

Housing Works Thrift Shops
multiple locations in NYC region
+ (347) 473-7400
www.housingworks.org

The Nest Store
online retail store
+ (866) 885-6584
www.theneststore.com

VivaTerra
online retail store
+ (800) 233-6011
www.vivaterra.com

INTERIOR DESIGN

Robin Wilson Home
New York, NY
+ (212) 863-9197
www.robinwilsonhome.com

INSULATION

Dow Building Solutions
local dealers nationwide
+ (866) 583-2583
www.building.dow.com

**Green Star Energy Solutions
(newspaper insulation)**
Brookfield, CT
+ (203) 744-1144
www.green-star-insulation.com

LEED VERIFICATION

Steven Winter Associates
offices nationwide
www.swinter.com

LIGHTING

Clodagh
New York, NY
+ (212) 780-5300
www.clodagh.com

Laura Lee Lighting Designs
Burbank, CA
+ (818) 842-5300
www.lauraleedesign.com

**Juno Lighting Group
(recessed LED lighting)**
local dealers nationwide
www.junolightinggroup.com

Oznium
online retail store
+ (866) 332-6411
www.oznium.com

Sandra Liotus Lighting Design
Newport, RI
+ (401) 845-9236
www.solatube.com

Solatube Passive Lighting Devices
local dealers nationwide
+ (888) 765-2882
www.solatube.com

MOVING COMPANY

JS Moving & Storage
New York & East Coast
+ (718) 418-6570
www.js-moving.com

Whalen's Moving & Storage Co.
Mt. Kisco, NY
+ (914) 241-3148
www.movewhalens.com

OUTDOOR

Vermont Castings (barbeque grilles)
local dealers nationwide
www.vermontcastings.com

**Jangir Maddadi Design Bureau
(concrete planters)**
Kalmar, Sweden
www.jangirmaddadi.se

Stiles and Hart Brick Company
Bridgewater, MA
+ (800) 320-8700
www.stilesandhart.com

PAINT

**Benjamin Moore & Co.
(maker of Aura paint)**
local dealers nationwide
www.benjaminmoore.com

PLUMBING, FIXTURES & EQUIPMENT

Kohler
local dealers nationwide
+ (800) 456-4537
www.kohler.com

Mr. Steam
local dealers nationwide
+ (800) 767-8326
www.mrsteam.com

Eternal Hybrid Hot Water Heaters
local dealers nationwide
+ (866) 946-1096
www.eternalwaterheater.com

RECYCLING

Green Demolitions
Greenwich, CT
+ (888) 887-5211
www.greendemolitions.com

Taylor Global Recycling Group
Montgomery, New York
+ (845) 457-4021
www.taylor-recycling.com

STONE & COUNTERTOP FABRICATION

Amendola Stone & Fabrication
White Plains, NY
+ (914) 997-7968
www.amendolamarble.net

SOLAR PANELS

SunPower/PowerLight
local dealers worldwide
+ (800) 786-7693
www.sunpowercorp.com

Mercury Solar Systems
Portchester, NY
+ (877) 643-8786
www.mercurysolarsystems.com

TECHNOLOGY

ADT Home Security
local dealers nationwide
+ (880) 720-8991
www.adt.com

Agilewaves
Menlo Park, CA
+ (650) 839-0170
www.agilewaves.com

Crestron
New York, NY
+ (516) 739-1010
www.crestron.com

TEXTILES

Laytner's Linen & Home
New York, NY
+ (800) 690-7200
www.laytners.com

Libeco-Lagae
New York, NY
+ (212) 764-1066
www.libeco.com

Melange Home
New York, NY
+ (212) 689-2002
www.melangehome.com

Mod Green Pod
Austin, TX 78756
+ (512) 524-5196
www.modgreenpod.com

The Nest Store
online retail store
+ (866) 885-6584
www.theneststore.com

Ralph Lauren (organic towels)
local showrooms nationwide
www.ralphlauren.com

VivaTerra
online retail store
+ (800) 233-6011
www.vivaterra.com

TILE & STONE

Chelsea Arts Tile + Stone
New York, NY
+ (646) 638-0444
www.chelseaartstileandstone.com

Dal-Tile Corporation
local showrooms nationwide
+ (214) 398-1411
www.daltile.com

ECO by Cosentino
local showrooms nationwide
+ (866) 579-4326
www.ecobycosentino.com

SPONSOR CREDITS

ADDITIONAL PHOTO CREDITS

Bill Mayo, Peter T. Michaelis, Scott Seifert, Kohler, John Yarema , Shad Gross, Robin Wilson, Eva Green